Hitch for 2011

NEVER BUILD A CAMPFIRE IN A HAYSTACK

Wake Maberry

Cover design by Bron Smith

Flaming Barn Press

Many of the names in this book have been changed to protect the innocent, even though they weren't innocent.

Never Build a Campfire in a Haystack

This book may be ordered through Lulu Books (www.lulu.com) or by contacting Wake Maberry at wakemaberry@gmail.com

ISBN: 978-0-615-58772-1

Dedication

This book is dedicated to my grandchildren:

Carter

Brett

Jaxon

Mallory

Braxten

Always Find Time to Laugh

Acknowledgements

To my wife, who has lived these stories…this book is proof that I still have difficulty completing assignments.

To my kids who have also lived these stories; they finally had to move away to start a normal life.

To my cousin, Bron, who always wanted me to write a book. He didn't say anyone would buy it. He just said I could write it.

To Cindy, whose critiquing was invaluable; you may come out of hiding now.

To Rick and Tom, and others who have given input; it is finished.

To everyone who has read my Christmas letters over the years, and encouraged me in this undertaking…thanks for your support.

Most people want to do something like this and don't; I didn't want to be that person.

About the Author

Wake continues to live in the town where he grew up, running from the big white rooster, burning down his Grandpa's barn, and frustrating teachers with his "wandering mind."

Growing up, Wake had a love for humor and writing. When his wife encouraged him to start doing a Christmas letter, he knew people didn't want to hear about his family's achievements, so he borrowed achievements from other families. The rest is history. Wake has been writing one-of-a-kind Christmas letters for the past 25 years. His wife has frequently threatened to publish them.

Through the years, those who've read his letters have urged him to write a book. His cousin, an author and illustrator, has frequently urged him with these words..."You can do it, but you've got to have gas in the tank and fire in the belly."

In his book, Wake talks about his shopping travails...and he has many. He hates shopping. To this day, he can't go to a store alone, without calling his wife to make sure he got it right.

He also writes about wrestling with Christmas trees, taking Christmas lights to the shooting range, trying to convince his mom that a dog was critical to his survival and, of course, the story that took the longest to find humor in...burning down his Grandpa's barn in the fourth grade. Hopefully, these stories and others will strike a humorous chord.

Wake is a former educator who now belongs to E.A....Educator's Anonymous. He's a recovering educator. As therapy, he and his wife, Connie, began leading people on tours throughout the United States and Canada.

Wake is a firm believer that laughter is great medicine. He hopes you'll be entertained by his look at life growing up...and even now.

He and his wife, Connie, live in Sequim, Washington. They have two children...who are trying to remain anonymous.

CONTENTS

Smoke in the Valley

Having just been paroled from *Helen Haller Elementary* for the summer, my cousin, Lester, and I were honing our skills as first class cowpokes at Gramps' Ranch, a large ranch located in the hills, about three miles above the town in which we lived.

We were attempting to break in a couple of horses, which were actually broomsticks with a cloth horse head.

It takes a highly skilled cowpoke to break in a wild broomstick. Unable to find one that was highly skilled, we had to break in our own broomstick. The results were not good. Our credibility as first-class cowpokes was badly damaged.

We decided to take a break in an old bull pen near the barn, and look at other occupations. We were extremely grateful the bull pen was empty, since bulls rarely listen to reason, and fail to see the humor of sharing their space with hapless cowpokes.

While several cows wandered over to offer their sympathies, I was telling Lester about a cow that set an entire city on fire.

"You're kidding!" he shouted in disbelief. "I hope they caught the cow that was responsible."

"No, no," I responded, "it was an accident. My teacher, *Miss Plumpinshort*, said a cow, belonging to one Mrs. O'Leary, kicked over a lantern in her barn. The lantern fell on some hay, which caught fire. The fire jumped to other nearby buildings, eventually spreading through the entire city. It was called the *Great Chicago Fire*. It happened in **1871**."

I could see Lester was impressed with my knowledge.

As we continued to nurse our bruises, and summon up enough courage to get back in the saddle, I was suddenly struck with a brilliant idea, possibly inspired by Miss Plumpinshort. "Hey, Lester, why don't we build a campfire?" "Besides," I went on, "real cowboys build real campfires. Why, you can't even tell a good story or sing a good song without a campfire."

"No wonder it's so quiet," answered Lester.

"Right...so let's start acting like real cowboys."

We found some rocks and placed them in a neat circle. In the middle of the circle, we placed some dry grass and bits of paper. Then we tried starting the fire using the Boy Scout method. We found two sticks and began rubbing them together. Nothing happened. "I think this only works if you're a Boy Scout," I said. So we tried banging two rocks together, but got more headache than spark.

"Maybe we need Mrs. O'Leary's cow," suggested Lester.

"I've got a better idea."

"What's that?"

"Matches," I replied.

"I don't know if that's a good idea," answered Lester. "Mom and Dad always tell us not to play with matches."

"Listen," I pleaded, "we're not playing. We're building a campfire. All cowboys have campfires."

After a little more encouragement and arm-twisting, Lester gave in to sound reason. "Once we get this fire going, we'll put that arm in a sling," I said.

Finding matches was our next priority.

"Why don't we ask your Mom and Grams for matches?" suggested Lester.

"No," I answered. "They're busy canning. They don't want to waste their time looking for matches."

Suddenly, I remembered seeing some matches in the house, in an upstairs bedroom. So I grabbed Lester and headed for the house. I sensed his reluctance as I pulled him along behind me, body rigid, and heels digging into the ground.

Not wanting to disturb anyone, I quietly shoved Lester through a back window, and then climbed in after him. He followed me upstairs and into the bedroom. As soon as we had gotten inside the door, I heard a muffled voice saying *"Psst! Over here...over here."* The voice was coming from inside a drawer across the room. Lester and I walked over to the drawer, opened it, and there were the matches. "Must be meant for us," I said rather matter-of-factly.

Taking the matches, we tiptoed quietly back downstairs and outside, being careful not to disturb Mom and Grams in their canning.

Once outside, we hurried back to our campsite in the bullpen, anxious to start our campfire; at least, I was anxious. Some of the cows had strolled over to watch, probably hoping we'd invite them in for a sing along. I took out one of the matches and struck it. Then I threw it into our circle of rocks. Nothing! I tried match number two, then three...four. Nothing! We'd gotten more heat banging two rocks together. I would have to come up with a better plan before I ran out of matches. "Maybe we should try some hay," I suggested.

"I don't know if that's a good idea," answered Lester, wrinkling his face and getting a bit fidgety.

"You're right," I said. "We'll just go to the barn. There's plenty of hay there; no use hauling it over here."

Lester was getting more skittish. So I sat on him for about fifteen minutes, until his nervous jitters subsided. Then he followed me to the barn, tugging at my shoulder, and almost dislocating it.

Arriving at the barn, we found it full of hay.

"This is perfect," I said, "There's just enough space to have a good campfire." I grabbed some loose hay and bunched it into a small pile. Hoping for better success than my previous attempts, I lit a match and threw it on the pile. The match was delighted! In less than a nanosecond, we had a roaring fire. Neither I, nor Lester, had planned for such success. An instant blaze was staring us in the face. We looked at the fire. Then we looked at each other and quickly decided on a plan of action---**PANIC!**

Not wanting to disturb anyone, we panicked as quietly as possible; standing frozen in our tracks, mouths hanging open, and eyes as wide as saucers. We considered fleeing the barn, but remembered you were never supposed to leave a fire unattended. That was a problem. There was no one else to watch the fire, and the cows had fled to the back forty with the smell of smoke.

I knew if we didn't take quick action, we were going to be *Cowboy Shish Kabob*. Since I had already passed on preventive action, our only choice was to smother the fire immediately. My eyes darted around the barn, looking for something I could use to smother it. There was nothing. All I could see was hay. So I grabbed a big pile and threw it on the fire. Bad decision! **NEVER** do that! The fire exploded into a roaring inferno!

"Let's get a blanket!" I yelled at Lester. "Maybe that will smother the fire."

"I've never seen a blanket that large!" he yelled back.

"Maybe we should roll on it!"

"Are you kidding!?" Lester yelled again. "I'm not going to roll on that!"

"It might be better than facing our parents!"

While we were considering our next move---disappearing into the deep, dark forest being one option---the fire was spreading rapidly, causing us to fear for our safety. With all the hay going up in flames, the cows had already resigned themselves to dining at the local feed lot.

Smoke was billowing out of the barn. We figured someone might suspect something, so we decided we would go to the house and get a bucket of water. The fire was far beyond the bucket-of-water stage, but we'd run out of other ideas.

We wanted to run and scream "**FFIIIIIRRRRREEEEE!!!**", but we knew that would cause alarm, so we practiced acting nonchalant.

After several rehearsals, we nonchalantly walked into the kitchen where Mom and Grams were busy canning, and talking about the increasing darkness.

"Looks like we're in for a bad storm," said Grams.

"Maybe worse than that," piped Lester.

"Sure seems odd," Mom said. "I haven't heard any thunder or seen any lightning, but I smell smoke."

I braced myself for a close encounter with lightning as I blurted out, "Could we have a bucket of water?"

It was a direct hit.

"Is the barn on fire?" asked Mom. I barely had "yes" out of my mouth, when nonchalant disappeared, and all the action went into fast-forward.

Grams instantly came down with a *"sick"* headache, and headed to the couch to lie down, while Mom ran to call the local fire department. Because we lived in a small town, it was an all-volunteer fire department. They usually did *"Fires by Appointment only."* Unfortunately, we hadn't scheduled the barn fire. I was hoping they would all volunteer. While Mom was on the phone, Gramps had seen the smoke and traced it to the barn with little trouble. He was now on his way to the fire carrying a bucket of water. I was just hoping he would look on the bright side. He could have a nice crop of roasted marshmallows.

Soon the fire truck arrived, but it was too late. As cars, filled with curious onlookers, began lining the road leading to the ranch, Lester and I went upstairs for a brief moment of quiet reflection, followed by a lengthy bout of hysterical sobbing. The fact that we had already outdrawn the carnival was of little solace.

In a bedroom, overlooking the blazing barn fire, we considered our future, or what was left of our future. It was possible that we had only a few hours to live. We figured our hides would be lying on the floor, on either side of Gramps' bear hide. In case our parents spared our lives, we calculated how long we would be in prison, with time off for good behavior---not starting anymore fires. We figured we might be allowed to see each other by the time we were in our late sixties.

For certain, we would go down in infamy as the two young boys responsible for the *Great Happy Valley Barn Fire.* Historians could not blame this one on a cow. The cows rejoiced, while Lester and I waited to see if we had a future beyond the fourth grade.

Rooster Rage

I've been pondering this for some time, and have finally come to the conclusion that every young boy should spend at least two years active duty on a farm. It would change his life forever. I know, because it changed my life forever. My wife says this is the very reason our friends don't want their children getting anywhere near a farm. They see what it did to me.

I must admit, I've never been the same since those years on Gramps' ranch. Although I survived dysfunctional cows, charging bulls and a burning barn, I have never fully recovered from rooster rage. I'm just now starting to eat on my own, and the nervous tics are beginning to disappear. But some nights I still find myself sitting on top of a split rail fence, sweating profusely, and gasping for air, waiting for someone to rescue me. When I wake up, I realize it's just a nightmare. Rudy is no longer with us.

Rudy was Gramps' big, white, demon-possessed rooster. He had little beady eyes and a slasher beak, to go along with his lethal talons. Judging from his size, I figure he must have been the first rooster on steroids.

My experiences with Rudy lead to years of trauma therapy. (My wife is still hoping I'll have a full recovery.)

For my cousins and me, Gramps' ranch was paradise. But to enjoy paradise, we had to go through torment. Torment was Rudy, the barnyard bully, who was meaner than a one-eared alley cat. He was always standing in our path to fun. It didn't matter which path we took. He was there, winking a beady eye and flashing his talons.

It was on the ranch that I learned to run like the wind. Rudy's day wasn't complete until he had me sprinting at Mach speed across the barnyard. After he had me nicely positioned atop a split rail fence, he would linger for a short while, taking a few pecks at the ground. Then he would strut off with that rooster swagger, looking for his next victim, while I looked for my next breath, and anxiously waited to be airlifted off the fence.

I used extreme caution anytime I set foot on Gramps' ranch. I would go through my usual routine: palpitating heart, sweaty palms, nervous twitching....At the same time, I would be surveying the landscape, looking for Rudy. Not seeing him, I would cautiously plant my feet in enemy territory. Then I would grab a nearby fence post to steady myself, and keep my wobbly knees from buckling. After gaining all the strength I could muster, I would rush the house under cover of heavy artillery fire. That was my fantasy. In reality, the only sound was the wind blowing through my hair, as I sprinted like a BB shot for the back door. Once inside, I would peek out the window. There would be Rudy, standing in the middle of the yard. When he saw me, he would wink a beady eye and flash one of his talons.

I tried to convince Gramps he was harboring an escapee from maximum security at *Fowl Feathers* poultry farm. No one was safe! I needed protection! "Could you hang a bell around Rudy's neck?" I asked. "Then I would know his whereabouts."

"That wouldn't be fair to Rudy," Gramps answered. "Besides, that running you do is good exercise." Then he would smile and continue reading his paper.

Anyone venturing onto the ranch unexpectedly would experience a close encounter of the mean rooster kind. It happened to my friend, Alan.

One morning he thought he would come by and ask if I could play ball. I happened to see him coming through the yard, whistling merrily as he made his way to the front door. I panicked. Alan was on rooster turf. I had no time to distract Rudy. It was too late. There was a sudden silence, followed by several shrieks that reverberated through the morning quiet. Looking out the window, I saw Alan roar by, followed closely by the "Evil" rooster. It appeared Alan might set a new land speed record for the barnyard, previously held by me. After zigzagging around numerous farm implements, and making several nice loops around the house, Alan spotted me holding the back door open. He roared in, huffing and puffing. I slammed the door shut.

"That was close," said Alan, badly shaken, but heaving a sigh of relief.

"At least he didn't get your lunch money," I answered.

Rudy was a Rooster Gone Berserk. I called it **Rooster Rage**. He didn't like the fact that chickens were disappearing. The chickens didn't like it, either. None of them wanted to be the next to have their picture on an egg carton, with a message asking if anyone had seen their whereabouts.

There were several predators in the area, but the most dangerous was Gramps. When it was time for a chicken dinner, he knew where to find the chicken. I had seen several on the dinner table. But I wasn't talking. With tension already running high, I was hoping Rudy wouldn't find out. I didn't want to be found bound and gagged in the hen house, with a ransom on my head. And I knew Rudy wouldn't be willing to exchange me for chicken on a platter. The prospect of having my youthful life come to an abrupt end in the hen house kept me quiet.

Oblivious to the escalating tension between Rudy and me, Gramps frequently said, "Wake, I want you to go out to the hen house and collect some eggs." The thought of venturing into that place sent chills down my spine.

"But Gramps," I'd plead, "I only collect baseball cards. Besides, I don't know anyone who trades eggs."

Gramps would shake his head and say, "My stars, I wonder if that boy will ever amount to anything."

I knew I would never amount to anything if Rudy caught me before I could start amounting.

I don't know why I was afraid to go into the hen house, because Rudy was never there. He was always roaming the barnyard, looking for me.

To go from the house to any other point on the ranch, you had to consider the possibility of a confrontation with the mad rooster, so I always tried to know his whereabouts before venturing outdoors.

Before leaving the house, I would go to every window, upstairs and downstairs, to pinpoint his location. I'd look out the front window. He was there! I'd look out the back window. He was there! I'd check the side window. He was there! I was surrounded!!

To get out, I would need to distract Rudy. I searched the house for grenade launchers, but found none. Deciding on a massive air strike, I ran upstairs, got out the water balloons, and filled them to the point of bursting. I was ready. I opened the window and started launching a full-scale attack. Rudy was running in circles, as my water bombs were splattering all around him. Finally, he disappeared. After a long silence, and not seeing him anywhere, I decided it was safe to make a break for it. No sooner had I stepped outside and shut the door, than Rudy magically appeared in all his radiant beauty, wings spread and flapping, preparing himself for a bodily assault.

Knowing it was my body he was preparing to assault, I quickly applied a geometrical truth...the shortest distance between two points is a straight line. Without hesitating, I roared off, with Rudy a close second. What I couldn't go over, under, or around, I went through. I must have lost Rudy in the poison ivy, because I didn't see him when I looked around.

Up ahead was the **Hen House of Doom**, not exactly a place of refuge, but far better than being out in the wide open spaces, with a crazed rooster-at-large. I ran in and slammed the door shut.

"Sorry ladies," I said. "Gramps sent me in here to collect some eggs."

I figured I might as well pretend I was amounting to something. I grabbed a half a dozen eggs and peered out through a crack in the door, hoping Rudy had given up and left the country.

What happened at that instant is rather vague, but I remember hearing a *cock-a-doodle-doo*, flapping wings, and seeing Rudy staring me in the face. Words were exchanged, followed by flailing arms and flying feathers. By the time I regained consciousness, I had crossed a river, run through a canyon, darted through the trees, and was sitting on top of a split-rail fence on the other side of the barnyard, covered with egg yolk and feathers. I don't know how long I straddled the fence, waiting for Search and Rescue, but Rudy finally lost interest and went swaggering back to the hen house, apparently pleased that he had been able to terrorize me once again.

I don't know if I'll ever amount to anything, but I owe my skills as an athlete to Rudy. He taught me to run like the wind---even with egg on my face.

When Cows Ruled

I was just looking out our living room window at the cows huddled together in the pasture below. It's such an idyllic setting. But I know these cows. They aren't waiting for a group picture, so they can be in the *"Cow Patty"* annual. They're involved in a strategy planning meeting. I suspect they're planning a fence-busting party. The farmer will probably get a call from a neighbor in the wee hours of the morning, letting him know that his cows have escaped, and are roaming the country roads, looking for trouble.

Growing up in a small town surrounded by dairy farms, I was well acquainted with the local cows; not that we spent a lot of time discussing the great *"cow movements"* throughout history.

Most of the time there was no fraternizing. Oh, there were a few cows that would chat with you over the fence, or gather around you in the pasture to hear your thoughts on cow healthcare.

Beyond that, most of them had their own agenda, and rarely listened to reason.

With cows far outnumbering the townspeople, farmers did their best to keep order. But it didn't take long for me to learn that cows ruled.

Their hooves left a lasting imprint on my life. I've tried to get it removed on several occasions, without success.

In the nearby hills, Gramps had a big ranch with a large herd of renegade cows. It was there that I learned one of the most important lessons in life---never trust a cow. You could never be sure which ones suffered from serious behavior disorders, such as kicking and butting, and an overwhelming desire to run over you. That's why I didn't like working with any cow unless I knew his complete work history. Was there any butting, kicking or stomping in his past? Was I dealing with an easy-going, level-headed slobber-master, or a cow that should be in lockdown?

As a kid, I often heard of contented cows, although I don't recollect ever meeting one in person. Growing up around cow gangs on the back forty, I was more acquainted with bovine malcontents, who were always grumbling and complaining about some perceived injustice. Gramps said they had probably spent too much time listening to Lester and me.

Sure, we may have whined occasionally about having to herd cows, but that was only because Gramps didn't require a criminal background check for any of his herd. You never knew when a cow would lead a breakout, and the whole herd would stampede over your body and through the valley, with no plans of stopping at 'grandma's house. We were putting our lives on the line.

You could hear murmurs of dissent, as Gramps' cows walked the fence line, feeling the pull of freedom, just beyond the barbed wire. They hated being fenced in while their cousins were roaming the open range, and basking in the glory of Hollywood westerns.

Many of their cousins had stomped their hooves on a Hollywood contract, and were now starring in cattle drives with John Wayne. Hollywood brought fame, especially if you were one of the leading cows, or a highly-sought-after stunt cow. You were recognized at every watering hole..."Hey, weren't you in that movie with John Wayne?"

"Oh, yeah...I'm surprised you recognized me with the hat and sunglasses."

These Hollywood celebrity cows were reaping the rewards of fat cow living; running with John Wayne not far behind, hanging out at the best watering holes, and doing commercials, encouraging everyone to eat more sushi. This was a far cry from the mundane life of the ranch.

Gramps finally had to break down and get a TV for the barn so the cows could watch their cousins in the westerns. They loved the stampedes. If you walked by the barn, you could hear them yelling, "Go the other way; the other way!", "Watch the rope!", "Don't pay any attention to the dog!" Another cow would pipe up, "Relax, it's just a movie."

Of course, their cousins would tell them it wasn't all watering holes and fat cow living. It was a lot of work, especially with all the re-takes. The director was always having them line up for another border run..."Alright, let's do the border run again, and let's stay together. If you get separated from the herd, let one of the cowboys find you. Don't wander off to some watering hole. And don't try to find the border on your own. You could end up in Vermont. If you're not certain which border you're crossing, ask one of the cowboys. They've got maps; any questions?"

Maybe life was better on the ranch. There was no fame. You were just a regular Joe cow. But there were no exhausting border runs.

Gramps' cows also got free entertainment, provided by Lester and me. Just watching us seemed to entertain them. Often they would wander over to where we were standing, and mill around, like they were waiting for the beginning of an outdoor concert.

One day, as Lester and I romped about the ranch on our horses, I came up with a brilliant idea. Brilliant ideas scared Lester. He started to run, but I grabbed him before he could get away. "Hold still and listen," I said. "We're not going to build a campfire." Lester breathed a sigh of relief. "Besides, there's no barn," I continued.

"Okay, what's your idea?" asked Lester nervously.

"Let's see if we can jump that split rail fence on our horses."

"We'd have to lower the fence," answered Lester, beginning to perspire.

"Okay, okay, maybe a couple rails," I responded.

We prepared the fence, and then we calculated the speed, timing of the jump, and clearance needed to get over the split rails. At the sound of a distant moo, we were off. About mid-flight we discovered that climbing over the fence would have been much easier. Trying to jump a fence while holding a broomstick between your legs took far more athleticism than either Lester or I possessed. We crash-landed, ending up with two very small horses, neither big enough to ride. It wasn't long before a number of cows had surrounded the crash site, staring in disbelief, and struggling to maintain their composure. After all, what would a cow look like, bent over, slapping a knee with a hoof, in raucous laughter? It wouldn't be cow-like.

Trying to preserve our bodies, Lester and I decided to ask Gramps if we could ride real horses. He just laughed. "I've got too much respect for horses to let you boy's on'em. I feel bad enough for those broomsticks." I'm sure that's why he had nailed the legs of his sawhorse to the floor. He probably thought Lester and I would try to ride it off into the sunset.

When we weren't entertaining the cows, we loved being entertained by westerns on TV. Gramps thought it was a waste of our time. "You boys don't need to be sitting in front of the TV all day, watching John Wayne move a bunch of trained movie cows, when you could be out helping me move cows that won't listen to anyone.

"But Gramps, what about our flawed character rubbing off on them?" I asked.

"Didn't you hear what I just said? They won't listen to anyone. Your flawed character has already rubbed off on them. That's why I need your help."

So we would shuffle reluctantly out the door, to help Gramps herd his behaviorally-challenged cows.

He was always moving them from pasture to pasture. Being close to a mathematical genius, I knew the shortest distance between two pastures was a straight line. If I had to herd cows, I wanted to walk the shortest distance...a straight line. The only problem---Gramps

15

cows fought straight lines. They would have none of it. When Gramps said, "Move'em out", cows would run into town for a cup of coffee, or maybe some Chinese food; anything to avoid a straight line. After dinner and a little window shopping, they would meander home, being sure to visit neighbors along the way.

Gramps was right! His cows didn't follow a script. They had learned well from Lester and me...always moseying off without telling anyone where they were going.

Herding Gramps' cows was no John Wayne cattle drive. It was hard work; something I much preferred watching others do. John Wayne was on horseback, moving cows that had been rehearsing border runs for months. They knew their roles well... stay with the herd...don't wander off....try to avoid stirring up too much dust. We were on foot, waving our arms wildly, and yelling in fluent cow (English was our second language), trying to move fence-busting renegades who were running in thirty-seven different directions.

There were always some that would sneak into the woods and hide, pretending to be lost. I would have to go in and negotiate their return to the herd. While I stumbled through the brush, looking behind the trees, I would hear a rustling sound, and some wise cow would charge out of the brush at me, pretending she was a bull (one of the games cows play), thus triggering my alarm system---highly sensitive from previous bull encounters---and causing me to high-step and jitterbug through the forest, screaming, "**BULL! BULL IN THE WOODS**!" Everyone else was yelling, "Stop! Stop! It's only a cow!" It was too late. After putting a great move on a couple tree stumps and jumping an irrigation ditch, I sprinted to safety. By the time Gramps found me, I was already at the house, two miles down the road; had eaten lunch, and was half-way through the sports page.

Herding Gramps' cows was perfect for developing speed, agility, and endurance, but I'd much rather turn on the T.V. and watch John Wayne do it on horseback. The cows agreed. And they ruled.

Take My Advice

I've always been told, "It's better to give than to receive." I agree. I find it far more enjoyable giving advice than receiving it.

During my school years, one of my favorite pastimes was giving advice to my cousin, Lester. With five younger sisters and two older parents, I figured Lester needed my advice if he was going to find any enjoyment in life. Okay, so my advice about building a campfire in a haystack didn't bring any joy. But that was just an isolated incident. Next time I would have better advice.

Being a year older, I felt I knew what was best for Lester. His father didn't share my feelings. He thought I should consider what was best for me. So I took his advice. I considered what was best for me; it was helping Lester.

One of his goals was to become rich, so he could retire to an island in the South Seas. It was either that, or senior housing in Fargo.

His mother didn't like his talk of riches. Every time Lester brought up the subject, she would say, "I'll slap your jaws." (This is really true! I'm not making this up!)

While his mother had Lester's jaws in her crosshairs, his father was always telling him to keep his chin up. "Hold your head high," he'd admonish Lester. I figured that would only put his jaws in line for a good slap.

Having Lester's interests at heart, and thinking I might profit from our friendship, I was willing to step in between his mother and his jaws, if necessary.

Having amassed a sizable fortune, myself, and knowing Lester wanted to become rich, I offered him my sage advice. "If you want to make more money than you've ever seen in your life---even more than lunch money, you can't walk around with your chin up and head held high," I said.

"Why not?" asked Lester, with a quizzical look.

"It's very simple," I answered. "First, your jaws are going to be in direct line of your slap-happy Momma. Secondly, money doesn't grow on trees; it falls out of pockets. Any financial genius, or anyone who plays 'kick the can,' knows money is on the ground: on sidewalks, in parking lots, and under carnival rides that turn you upside down. So take my advice; keep looking down, because the money is on the ground."

Lester was a bit hesitant to take my advice, claiming he hadn't fully recovered from the barn incident. "Forget the barn," I said. "We're talking riches here."

Since that was Lester's dream, he decided my advice was the best he'd heard since the barn went up in smoke. So he began walking everywhere with his head down, knowing it would be only a matter of time before he became filthy rich. After giving me a small percentage---say fifty percent---for my advice, he could then fulfill his dreams of early retirement in Fargo...I mean the South Seas.

I think Lester would have enjoyed life on a tropical isle, but a bizarre incident caused his plans to take a detour. It happened one morning on the school playground. He and a friend were walking along, playing kick-the-can, and discussing the latest financial trends, when they both spotted some money on the ground in front of them. Visualizing life in the South Seas, Lester ran for the money. At the last minute, his friend pushed him aside. As Lester looked up, one of his front teeth collided with a tetherball pole. The tooth fell to the ground. Lester's vision of the South Seas became blurred, as his finances trended below the horizon. He did receive a new, shiny gold tooth, but his father wasn't happy. He thought Lester should have been paying attention to where he was going.

I felt Lester was paying full attention to where he was going; after the money on the ground. He had no idea that a tetherball pole would suddenly rise up out of the ground and knock his tooth out.

Not wanting to ruin the fragile relationship I had with his father, I decided to keep a low profile while Lester recovered from the trauma.

It wasn't long before Lester was back to his old self; listening to my advice.

"I would cut across the field to Gramps," I told him. "It's quicker than walking around the pasture."

"I don't know," said Les, squirming a bit. "What about the bull?"

"What bull?"

"The bull that's always in the field," said Les.

"Do you see the bull?"

"No, but I still think I should go around."

"That will take thirty minutes; well, at least ten minutes," I said. "Besides, I'm sure Gramps moved the bull to another pasture."

Realizing he could save time, Lester took my advice. He climbed over the fence and stepped into the field of high grass.

I told Lester to save me a spot in one of Gramps' cherry trees. I would be over shortly. Lester was glad he had taken my advice. Now he could beat me to the best cherries.

Sitting on the fence, I watched him intently as he trekked across the field. As I continued watching, something in the distance caught my eye. It was the bull! He was lying down in the grass. I yelled..."Lester, STOP! The bull is lying down just ahead of you! **Back slowly and exit quickly**!" Translated, this means *"run for your life!"* At the same time, Lester and the bull spotted each other. The bull stood up to welcome Lester. But Lester wasn't going to the party.

They stared at each other across the high grass. Fearing the worst, I ran around the pasture to meet Lester on the other side. As I ran, I kept an eye on the unfolding drama.

Lester was studying the bull's body language. The bull was studying Lester's body. Suddenly, he lurched forward. Lester quickly reasoned that the bull's body language indicated there wasn't enough time to back slowly, so he skipped that part, and went straight to *"run for your life!"* Adrenaline shot through his body like water through a fire hose. Lester vividly remembers it as the **Great Adrenaline Rush**.

I was impressed by Lester's jaw-dropping speed. Racing across the field, toward the farmhouse, with the bull in pursuit, Lester knew the only exit would be over the fence. But the fence arrived sooner than expected. Just before he hit it on the dead run, he made a valiant leap. He would have cleared the fence easily if he hadn't gotten hung up in the barbed wire. Lester slowly pulled himself over the top and dropped to the ground, where I was waiting.

"What are you doing here?" he groaned.

"I ran around," I answered. "I thought you might need some help."

"You can help me count puncture wounds."

"Yeah, it looks like you should have waited for the bull. It would have been less painful."

I helped Lester into the house. After soaking in a tub of Epsom salts for a couple of hours to soothe his wounds, Lester joined me in the cherry tree. I had some more advice for him, but I thought I'd better let him get some nourishment first.

As we gorged ourselves on cherries, we kept an eye on the irrigation ditch that ran by the orchard. Our parents had warned us about the ditch walker. They said he loved catching little kids who were playing in the ditch. We thought playing in the ditch was worth the risk.

We had never seen a picture of the ditch walker, but we envisioned a Troll in waders. Rumor had it that, if we were caught, the ditch walker would whisk us away to a remote, undisclosed location, where we would be held for hours and forced to recite our multiplication tables. It sounded a lot like after-school detention. We pictured ourselves on our knees, begging the ditch walker not to ask us the answer to seven times eight. This caused us to be ever vigilant, lest we fall into the hands of the evil Troll in waders. I suspect if the ditch walker had been a teacher with a homework assignment, we wouldn't have gotten within five miles of the ditch.

After we'd thrown up all the cherries we'd eaten (according to our parents, this was a requirement for eating too many cherries), we climbed down to play in the ditch. I suggested to Lester that he go upstream and keep a lookout for the ditch walker while I played. Not long after, Lester came floating by. "It's a good thing you're holding on to that branch," I said, as I pulled him out. "This is no time for a float trip. Now cough up the rest of that water while you're lying here on the bank. Your dad would probably think it was my idea to send you up the ditch alone."

Suddenly, we heard squeals. We were certain it was the ditch walker with a little kid under each arm. We took off in search of new lands or, at least, a place to hide until we knew it was safe to come out. We listened intently, as we peeked out from behind some bushes. We thought we heard someone pleading, "No, No, not nine times six. Please, can we do the two's?" Then we heard more squealing. "Yikes, they're into forced fractions," I winced. All of a sudden, Gramps crossed the ditch, carrying two squealing piglets that had run off. We breathed a sigh of relief. Once again we had escaped the ditch walker. We could go back to playing in the ditch, maybe even float a couple homework assignments. We could always blame the dog.

After dinner, Grams invited Lester and me to spend the night. Although we loved spending the night on the Ranch, you always had to be prepared for *"The Call." "The Call"* meant cows were on the loose.

This is why Gramps needed guard towers with strobe lights for the pasture. Cows standing together in a group are not waiting for the bus. They're planning a big escape. And they never escape during the day. They escape only at night, preferably in a driving rainstorm, when you're playing checkers by the fire, or you're sound asleep.

21

That night Gramps got *"The Call."* "You've got some cows out," Gramps' distant neighbor, Mr. Franski, said. "It looks like the **Great Cow Escape**."

"Wake up boys," yelled Gramps. "I've got some cows out. And don't forget your slickers. There's a driving rainstorm."

We stumbled out of bed and put on our rain gear. Then we jumped into Gramps' pickup and rushed over to the scene of the crime.

As soon as Gramps issued the call to arms, we jumped out of the truck and began waving our arms wildly. We shouted at the cows to put down their luggage and line up along the fence. Then I began giving Lester some advice, trying to get him in position so no cows would escape. Just as I had Lester in position, and had told him to hold his ground, a cow bolted from the group, apparently attempting a run for the border. As the cow came barreling toward Lester, I feared Lester might attempt to outrun the cow to the border, so I yelled again, "**Hold your ground**!" In that instant, Lester dove out of the way as the cow romped past. "I didn't want to hold the ground that close," he said, getting to his feet. Lester had just ignored my advice. His dad would've been proud.

After some lengthy negotiations and tough cow talk, the escapees returned.

Lester and I walked the fence line on our way back to the house. Along the way, we spotted a large opening; just large enough for a cow to walk through. "Just what I suspected, "I said.

"What did you suspect?" asked Lester.

"I figured we'd find an opening large enough for a cow to walk through."

"The perfect escape route," Lester answered.

We spent the rest of the night helping Gramps mend the fence, and looking for other possible escape routes. When we were finished, I said, "Lester, we need to go home and get some sleep before we spend another day on the Ranch."

"Good advice," answered Lester.

Dancing with Flames

I was hunkered down in my recliner recently, doing some stretching exercises. As I was going into my third yawn, the dancing flame of a burning candle caught my attention. There's something mesmerizing about a flickering flame. As I stared at the flame, I thought about the magnetic appeal fire has on a man.

I've read that man's attraction to fire is part of a deeply-rooted instinct to try and master it. The article stated that those who don't master fire at an early age will be more attracted to it as an adult, possibly why the flame had lured me into a seductive trance.

The article didn't say how old a man had to be before he realized mastering a fire would never happen.

As I continued to stare at the flickering flame, it re-kindled memories of a glorious childhood. Then there was my own childhood, when I danced with flames.

I didn't want you to put me on a pedestal, so I wasn't going to mention my past. But I was once a firefighter. In fact, I come from a long line of firefighters. Well, I don't know if the line was that long. Now that I think about it, the line was very short. It was primarily my cousins and me, who fought fires during our youth.

Like most kids, whose dream is to become a firefighter, we felt a strong bond with fire at an early age. Of course, learning to fight fires required the use of an actual fire. You couldn't fight a fire unless you had a fire to fight. And you couldn't go out and borrow someone else's fire. So we figured the only way to learn was to start our own.

We found a number of vacant lots and old orchards nearby, with plenty of dry grass that provided the perfect training ground for us to learn our firefighting skills.

I can still remember my own two legs driving furiously up and down like two well-oiled cylinders, as I attempted to stomp out any remaining fire in the dry grass of a vacant lot. My cousins and I called it *"Dancing with Flames."*

By the age of twelve, we were self-made firemen. We had put out more fires than most veteran firefighters. Any one of us could've qualified as Fire Chief. Our camaraderie was strengthened by a common bond: We smelled like smoke. We thought it was an air freshener.

Our ability to start a fire led some to believe that just our standing in a vacant lot could cause the entire lot to burst into flames.

Most of us believed a fire was a rite of passage from youth to adulthood, although my campfire in a haystack almost caused me to miss the passage to adulthood.

During the summer, when we had more time to polish our skills, the local fire department was always on standby. There was even some talk of building a fire lookout in our neighborhood, but the petition was invalidated because several neighbors had signed multiple times.

Although we felt we were accomplished firefighters, **Farley Barnsmell**, the local sheriff, didn't hold us in the same high regard.

He viewed us with suspicion. Just seeing us standing by a vacant lot would cause him to twitch and shake.

During our training, we learned that failure to stomp out a fire meant dealing with Farley, and he didn't enjoy fireside chats. He never believed us when we told him the fire was started by some mysterious *"bush."* He would make a big fuss about the danger to nearby homes. Then he would lay out the detention center scenario, which we had memorized. It was much easier putting out the fire and scattering.

On occasion, fire would sneak up on us when we were least expecting it. It happened to Lester. One hot summer day, he discovered a nest of earwigs had taken up residence in an old mattress, in the orchard behind his house. He realized he would have to take a stand since the mattress was his bed when he camped in the orchard.

So he decided to turn up the heat on the earwigs. He grabbed his magnifying glass and went to work. With a steady hand and fierce concentration, he had the earwigs fleeing the mattress.

Having subdued them, he went back into the house, assuming the matter was finished. That was until his mom heard the sirens and saw a fire truck pull up outside the house. Lester had applied too much heat. The smoldering mattress had burst into flames. The dry grass around the mattress had caught fire, and was threatening the orchard and nearby homes.

As he watched the smoke curl into the sky, Lester thought it would be a good time for a change of address. Disguising himself as a nun, and joining a convent, was another option. But it was too late. His father had just arrived home from work. He promptly turned up the heat on Lester. Lester did his version of *Skip-To-My-Lou*.

He was banned from possession of a magnifying glass until he was twenty-one. His parents considered it a firearm.

Of course, the ever-plotting Lester was still considering his options. He thought he should get a new mattress in exchange for the magnifying glass. After several weeks, he presented the idea to his parents. They agreed, as long as Lester kept the mattress on his bed.

During the summer our imaginations ran on overload. The neighbors were always on *"high"* alert. They were prepared for the Apocalypse.

One summer day, my imagination came up with a brilliant idea, something I would never have thought of, myself. "Let's make fire fly!" I said excitedly.

"We can't make fireflies," said my friend, Ernie.

"Not fireflies," I answered. "Let's make fire fly. Let's make a home-made hot air balloon."

"How are we going to make a hot air balloon?" asked Ernie.

"All we need is the right material and a little fire," I answered.

"A little fire shouldn't be a problem," said Ernie. "If we can find the right material, I'm sure a little fire will rush right over."

Our first stop was the nearby dry cleaners. They were more than happy to supply us with several dry cleaning bags for our clandestine operation. They seemed oblivious to the fact they were aiding and abetting the soon-to-be notorious *"**Hot Air Balloon Gang**."*

Later that evening, we marveled at our own creativity as we assembled our balloons. Once assembled, a little fire rushed right over, just as Ernie had prophesied. We held the balloons while they filled with hot air. Soon they began to lift off. After they were high in the sky, drifting over town, we called city hall and reported strange, unidentified flying objects crossing overhead.

Then we ran over to the main highway. There was a lonely car coming through town. Seeing a driver behind the wheel, we positioned ourselves alongside the road and looked upward, pointing to the sky. The driver stopped and got out. Looking up, he marveled at the strange, glowing objects, passing silently overhead. Then he jumped back in his car and sped away, probably fearing an alien invasion.

Considering the possibility of a crash burn, we always followed our balloons on foot or in someone's car. We didn't want a stray balloon reducing the town to smoldering timbers. Having already spent years on the run from teachers, we didn't like the thought of spending the rest of our lives as fugitives.

One evening we were following one of our balloons in a friend's car, when it landed in flames, in an open field near town. We rushed to the field, where we performed our signature rendition of the "*Grass Fire Stomp*." (I'm surprised that little dance didn't land us a spot on American Bandstand.) By the time Farley, the human smoke detector, arrived, we were long gone, preparing another hot air balloon for lift off.

One warm summer evening, around midnight, Lester and I decided to send up a hot air balloon from my backyard. We got everything together, assembled the balloon, and prepared for lift-off. We always considered wind, so our balloons would clear homes in the neighborhood as they would drift off into the night sky.

This night our plans took a detour. As soon as we had launched our balloon, we realized that we had misjudged the breeze. We were looking at potential disaster. The balloon was on a direct line for the neighbor's roof antenna. We tried "coaxing" it in another direction, but I could hear the balloon say, *"Forget it! I'm going for the antenna! Ha...ha...ha! You're going to be in big trouble now."* It never veered off course. We stared at the ball of fire hanging from the antenna while our future was, again, hanging by a thread. "I think we're almost out of thread," opined Lester.

I agreed with the balloon. "This could be big trouble," I said, pummeled by flashbacks of a burning barn.

If the ball of fire fell to the roof, the remainder of our years would be in jeopardy.

Not wanting to disturb the neighbors with fire trucks and sirens, we chose our best *"life extension"* option; quietly and quickly, **very quickly**, get a water hose and put out the fire. After the *barn fire*, the *mattress fire*, the *ant hill fire*, and all the control burns that we needed help controlling, Farley didn't need to know about the *"antenna fire."*

Rounding up a hose, we pointed it at the flaming antenna and turned it on full force. With the stars shining brightly in a cloudless sky, we were hoping the neighbors wouldn't wake up and become suspicious of the deluge pounding their roof. If they found out their roof was on fire, they wouldn't like the surprise.

Just when we had extinguished the fire, a car stopped. The driver got out. "What are you boys doing?" the man asked.

"Watering the flowers," Lester said in a low voice.

"It seems a bit late for watering flowers," the driver continued.

"It's too hot during the day," I responded, as convincingly as possible.

"Yeah...well, you're not going to water too many flowers with that hose pointed at the roof."

"Oh, you're right," said Lester, as he lowered the hose. "Your stopping to chat must have distracted me. Thanks for bringing that to my attention." The fellow drove off, shaking his head.

Thinking he might call Farley, we quickly turned off the hose. Then we disappeared into the house. Moments later we peeked out the window and spotted Farley prowling the area, probably making sure the flowers were watered.

The next day, mom was talking to the neighbors. "Did it rain last night?" Mr. Snow asked.

"I don't think so," Mom answered.

"It sounded like we had a heavy downpour, but I don't see any evidence of it this morning," Mr. Snow continued.

While they were talking, Mom happened to glance up and see the remnants of the hot air balloon hanging from the antenna. "It was probably just an isolated shower," she told Mr. Snow.

When Mom came back into the house, she said, "Well, boys, it looks like one of your hot air balloons didn't make it out of the neighborhood. I just hope I don't have to explain that one to Mr. Snow." We hoped so, too.

A number of years have passed since the *"Flaming Antenna"* incident, but we still get together on occasion and reminisce about our years as firefighters.

I'm surprised we've never been recognized with a nice plaque, commemorating our years of service. Maybe it's because we started most of the fires. But how else would we learn to fight fires?

Booger Tales

A dog is man's best friend. Everyone needs a best friend.
I did the math. Math doesn't lie. I needed a dog.

Growing up as an only child in our home, I would enjoy the
companionship, and I would learn responsibility. I just had to
convince my mother that a dog was critical to my well-being. That
wouldn't be easy. Unlike most sensible dog lovers, Mom was not
impressed with shedding hair, disemboweled sofas, and half a
slipper, not to mention lawn fudge.

Every time I mentioned the need for a dog in my life, Mom turned
a deaf ear to me. So I tried her good ear; same result.

"How about a girlfriend in place of a dog," I suggested one day, in
desperation.

"You're too young to be thinking about girls," she answered
adamantly.

I knew I was too young to drive, but I had no idea there was an age
limit on thinking about girls. "How old do I have to be for a permit?"
I asked.

"For you, I would say, at least 35."

I would have to fight that battle later. Right now I had to focus on getting a dog. Trying to convince Mom that a dog was an absolute necessity would require some hand-wringing appeals, along with some possible blood-letting.

Before I could make my first emotional, hand-wringing appeal, Mom tried the *"appeasement"* trick. "I've decided it would be good for you to have a pet," she proclaimed one morning.

My face lit up! "Wow, does that mean a dog?"

"Not at all," she answered, "we're getting two parakeets."

My face darkened. *"Are parakeets going to flush out quail?"* I mumbled to myself. *"Of course not,"* I continued to mumble.

I checked the calendar for the opening of hunting season on parakeets. There was none. I went back to the strategy room.

While I was devising a plan to have a dog miraculously appear at our front door, mom was keeping a watchful eye for any dogs that might lose their way and stray into our yard.

If a dog lost its way, Mom would meet it with a curled lip and a snarl. Frightened, the dog would bolt for the neighbor's yard. I would bolt for the neighbor's yard.

Her goal was to get dogs added to the endangered species list; my goal was to own one before they became extinct.

I would have to plan my strategy well if I was ever going to have a dog. This would require cunning and perseverance, something that comes easily to most kids.

Since mom disliked anything with four legs, I decided to try the *modified approach.* "Okay," I said, "I'm willing to settle for a three-legged retriever. I don't care if he limps. He can chase decoys." Mom would hear none of it.

I proceeded to the *guilt strategy.* "But Mom, all the kids in the neighborhood have a dog."

"Ernie is the only kid in the neighborhood," Mom answered.

"I know…and he has a dog." I didn't think it was necessary to add frivolous details like his dog's dining habits: shoes, furniture, electrical cords…

"Does Ernie's dog clean up after himself?" Mom asked.

"I don't recollect ever seeing a self-cleaning dog," I answered.

"Exactly," Mom said. "And who do you think would be cleaning up after your dog?"

"Obviously it would be you," I answered.

"That's a good reason not to have a dog," said Mom.

"Okay," I pleaded, "I'll train him to go in the neighbor's yard. I promise."

Mom shot me a look of displeasure that glanced off my forehead, leaving me momentarily dazed. Another shot like that and I would have to hunker down behind some furniture.

I could see this wasn't going to be easy. Mom's well-thought-out rebuttals would be hard to penetrate. Hopefully, my pouting, whimpering and whining would overcome her sound reason.

As she continued presenting her case for not having a dog, I excused myself and high-tailed it for Ernie's.

"Maybe you should try a different approach," suggested Ernie. "Why don't you start out with a rental dog?"

"Are you **KIDDING**?" I asked.

"No, you could rent a dog for special occasions, like when you just need a companion for the day, or to run off meter readers, tax assessors, or other vermin."

It wasn't a bad idea, but I really wanted my own dog.

I went back home to plan my next move. Mom's reasoning was taking a toll on me. She had me pinned against a wall. Then I remembered the *"floor flop"* approach. This approach involves falling to the floor and thrashing about wildly, interspersed with moments of loud wailing, until your Mom says, *"Okay, okay, you can have a dog."* I knew this approach had been highly successful for many children over the years. But after prolonged consideration, I decided against it. My back was still too sore from being pinned against the wall.

Looking for someone with tremendous wisdom and keen insight, I turned to Ernie's dad for counsel. "Owning a dog is a big responsibility," he said. "It won't be easy for someone who isn't

31

responsible." I ignored his irrational comment and forged ahead toward my goal.

Mom's favorite words were *"Scat,"* *"Shoo,"* and *"Get out of here,"* but I refused to leave. I was determined to stand my ground until victory was at hand.

If I used a little sound reason of my own, I knew I could help mom overcome her blind spot and see the real joy of pet ownership.

I carefully explained how caring for a dog would teach me responsibility. Mom was overcome with mirth. "If you take care of him like you take care of the parakeets, he'll starve to death," she said.

Not being one to give in to absolute truth, I resorted to a little *adolescent diplomacy*...crying, carrying-on, and threatening to run away. Seeing my level-headed approach, Mom finally agreed to give it a try. There was only one stipulation. She insisted that Obedience Training School be a part of the deal. I grudgingly accepted.

Soon I had a shiny, black, Labrador retriever. I would have been better off with a stuffed bear. Anyway, I named him Booger.

Now I had to uphold my end of the deal--Obedience Training School. At the end of the first session, I was impressed! *"Why didn't I bring Booger?"* I asked myself. Within an hour, I had learned to "sit." Mom would be pleased. The most difficult session was learning to come when I was called. (My wife says I'm still struggling with that concept.) Like I've told her, a dog biscuit is not my idea of a reward.

During the final session, I learned heeling; walking nicely by Booger's side. Mom was getting more than her money's worth. I was already learning responsibility.

Housebreaking Booger was my next goal. But as soon as I let him in the house, he did the housebreaking. His tail was a whirling dervish. The living room became an arcade. Judging from the **WPS**, (*wags per second*) he was determined to knock over as many knick-knacks as possible and win a stuffed animal.

After all the effort I had put forth to get a dog, Booger was not starting out on the right paw.

Trying to grab knick-knacks and his tail at the same time, I pictured both of us stuffed, hanging side by side over the mantle.

With winter fast approaching, our fortunes changed. Mom said she had postponed our date with the taxidermist. Booger and I breathed a sigh of relief.

Although she questioned their existence, Mom hated to see any dog out in the cold. I hoped for a long, cold winter. It finally happened. One cold night she said Booger could stay in my room. Mom carefully guarded her knick-knacks as Booger loped through the living room, happily wagging his tail.

Booger hadn't eaten, so Mom gave me his bowl and some hamburger. "You need to feed that dog," she said. I figured eating out of a bowl all the time had to be boring, so I decided to make it fun for Booger. I rolled up some hamburger into a little ball and threw it into the air. Booger jumped up and grabbed it. I repeated the procedure. Same result. The third time I threw the hamburger too high and, to my amazement, it stuck to the ceiling. I looked at the meat on the ceiling. At the same time I thought I heard *"responsible ownership"* sneaking out the window. I began throwing little balls of hamburger in the air until the ceiling looked like a meat market. Hearing Booger whining, Mom came in and saw him looking up, staring at *"Hamburger Heaven."*

"It looks like *'responsible ownership'* has gone out the window," said Mom.

"Yeah, I guess I should shut it before anymore tries to leave."

I could sense impending doom. It arrived sooner than I expected. "After this hamburger returns to earth, you can get some soap and water, and clean the ceiling," she continued. "Then, since you love camping, you and Booger can trade places tonight."

After scrubbing down the ceiling, I grabbed my sleeping bag and trudged out the door. As I bedded down for a long, cold night, Booger was enjoying my warm bedroom. He would occasionally look out the window with a big smile and wave. I was too numb to wave back.

Booger quickly earned a reputation as a highly-skilled and discriminating retriever. When I think of retrieving, I'm thinking birds. Booger and I didn't think alike. He had no interest in birds.

I tried taking him duck hunting, but he was a lousy shot. He did manage to round up a decoy, but I told him to leave them alone; they were too hard to clean.

Booger's specialty was *"Clothesline Clothes Removal."* He would only go on point at the sight of clothes hanging from a clothesline. I could throw a ball or a stick for him to fetch, and he would turn up his nose in contempt. But someone across town could hang a negligee out to dry in the middle of the night, and it would arrive at our doorstep before the morning paper.

While I was at school, Booger was laying waste to the neighborhood. Clotheslines were stripped of stockings, underclothes, pants, and any shirts that fit. If there was a stray shoe on the porch, he would grab it. (I'm surprised he didn't break out windows and set fire to homes.)

Then he would deposit his collection around the yard. He seemed to find particular joy in leaving all the undergarments on the front porch.

Best friends don't leave undergarments on your front porch. So I told everyone he was a stray that I had befriended. I hardly knew the dog.

School became an unlikely place of refuge. The dismissal bell sent shivers galloping down my spine. That meant it was time to go home, and I didn't want to go home. Going home meant answering knocks at the door, and matching up Booger's *clothesline collection* with the right neighbors. Each day I sensed growing opposition to Booger. My own life was at risk. I feared people throwing rocks and chanting for their clothes.

I would have preferred being locked up in isolation with algebra.

Booger was looking more and more like a rental dog.

Certainly, a hardened criminal on the run would have been an easier boarder.

After broken knick-knacks, waiting for hamburger to return to earth, and finding more clothes in our yard than she had in her closet, mom said the experiment was over. Besides, most of the clothes didn't fit. She also wanted her friends to return.

Having an irresponsible dog was worse than having an irresponsible son. The only thing Booger had taught me was to leave my clothes in the yard.

Some suggested I leave Booger on someone's doorstep, but I didn't want to destroy another family. It would take some time to calculate the damage to our own family.

If you've never owned a dog, try renting one first. On second thought, take the stuffed bear.

As the Mind Wanders

I love the sounds of spring: April showers dancing on the roof, birds happily singing, my wife and I crashing through the attic, looking to uncover priceless gems that will draw countless thousands or, at least, the neighbors to our annual spring garage sale.

This spring a real treasure caught my eye. After a few eye drops, I could see it was my old report cards. *"Yikes! How did they find their way into the attic?"* I asked myself. I thought they had mysteriously disappeared in a grass fire years earlier, or had floated down an irrigation ditch to the ocean, and had washed ashore in another country, only to be denied entrance. Instead, they loomed in front of me, like Miss Hatchet with a paddle in her holster. I quickly grabbed hold of something to steady myself.

I had done my best to hide them from my children, not wanting them to know the darker side of my life. Now they would find out about *math, biology, woodshop, Miss Hatchett,* and other destructive influences in my life.

My wife picked up one of my report cards and looked inside. Under comments she read, *"Has difficulty completing assignments."*

"I have an excuse...I mean an explanation for that," I said. "How can you complete something that's been swept away in an irrigation ditch or reduced to ashes in a grass fire?"

"That reminds me...did you remember to take out the garbage?" Connie asked.

"I was going to, but you distracted me with this project."

"Still has difficulty completing assignments," she muttered to herself.

Connie continued to the next comment..."*Mind wanders.*" "That hasn't changed," she muttered again. "Where is it now? I know it's not on the garbage, because it's still waiting to be taken out. It's getting restless."

"Okay, okay, I was just on my way to escort it to the curb."

"I can see why school was such a challenge. Your body may have been there, but your mind had already retired."

"That wasn't my fault," I answered. "Our school didn't offer anything in its area of interest...the art of climbing cherry trees, how to float homework in an irrigation ditch, how to outwit a demented rooster, and dating. It once joined me for algebra, but Mr. Rottweiler gave it a case of the *"fits."* It spent a short time with me in woodshop, but I made it too nervous, being so close to power tools.

I was glad I could finally explain my side of the report card. My teachers always seemed to turn a deaf ear when I tried to explain to them that they were putting my mind at risk, and that I couldn't be held responsible for any of its actions.

Although I loved going to school to escape from my dog, school was never my first choice. It wasn't my teachers' first choice for me, either. Most of them didn't like the fact that my mind and I rarely came to school together. While I was at school, it would be roaming wild and free, rafting across Gramps' lake, catching frogs, climbing cherry trees, or chasing roosters (just a fantasy I had).

If I could have gotten my mind to come to school more often, I'm certain I could have made the honor roll. Gramps didn't think I needed that much to make it. He was always telling me, "You could make the honor roll if you had half a mind to." Unfortunately, I had a hard time getting half a mind to school.

When I did, my teachers would try to convince me I could do the work if I would put my mind to it." It sounded simple, but putting half a mind to anything is no easy task.

My mind and I would try to connect on occasion, but it was usually after school and during the summer. We rarely connected during class. This increasingly irritated my teachers.

"Mr. Maberry, has your mind taken another leave of absence?" Mr. Bagley would ask. "Why don't you go out in the hall and see if you can find it."

After allowing me sufficient time to scour the hallways, he would call me back into the room. "Well, Mr. Maberry, did you find it?"

"No, but I think I can tell you where it is," I answered. Everyone suddenly stopped what they were doing and listened. Kids walking by the room stopped in their tracks. The clock stopped. Time stood still.

Mr. Bagley finally spoke. "Okay," he asked, "Where is it?"

"It's been kidnapped," I said. Everyone stared in disbelief. After all, who would want my mind; it never stuck around long enough for much good.

"Who's the unlucky one?" asked Mr. Bagley.

"Sally," I answered.

The silence was shattered by a deafening roar. After restoring order to the class, he said, "I think you need to get your mind off Sally and let English captivate your mind." I tried, but Sally was much more captivating.

It wasn't long before my mind was off on another sightseeing venture.

Every so often it would show up in class and startle me. One day it stopped by my general math class to show me some pictures it had taken while vacationing in Cancun. While I was looking at the pictures, my counselor stepped into the class and announced, "Mr. Maberry, you need to be in algebra." For a brief moment I thought it was a promotion, but my mind was waving a red flag. Trusting my mind, I felt an evil foreboding. The future didn't look good, either.

The next day I found myself sitting in Mr. Rottweiler's algebra class. It wasn't where I wanted to find myself. I would have preferred Disneyland.

I soon understood the red flag. It was Mr. Rottweiler. He was short, stocky and gruff. Mixing him with algebra was like throwing a match on gasoline. I looked around the room at the other students. I wondered how many of us could survive multiple explosions. My desk would offer little protection. I would have to convert it into a walled fortress.

I was now a **P.O.A**. (*Prisoner of Algebra*) in this little class of math horrors. I was constantly being harassed by menacing algebra problems. "I think algebra may be a violation of the *Geneva Convention*," I mentioned one day.

"You think so, huh?" questioned Mr. Rottweiler, biting off a piece of chalk and spitting it out. "Well, we'll see what the Geneva Convention has to say about me sending you to the blackboard, to solve all those problems."

Anyone who was deficient in solving for x faced his wrath. I was beyond deficient. I was anemic. With no help from the Geneva Convention, I tried to save myself. I could smell the air of freedom when I heard the voice of Mr. Rottweiler..."Mr. Maberry, *get out of that window*! If we were on the second floor, I would let you jump. Now return to your seat!"

I tried to convince him that I wasn't ready for algebra, and might never be ready, but he just ignored my feigning insanity and the drool running down the front of my shirt. "Mr. Maberry," he said, "you can do algebra if you put your mind to it."

First of all, I never knew if my mind was going to be on location. Secondly, it had to be willing to participate. Any contact with algebra would often cause it to have spells of "*fits*."

Dad tried to help. He bought me a book called *Algebra Made Simple.* I would have preferred *Campfires Made Simple*. I quickly discovered that the word "*Simple*" was just a teaser to get people to open the book. I scoured every page, from front cover to back cover. I found nothing simple. It had completely disappeared. I considered bringing in a team of experts, to see if they could locate it, but decided I would have to stand alone against the force of darkness...algebra.

To shield my eyes from Mr. Rottweiler's blinding glare, I tried holing up in the back of the class, behind the tallest and widest student available.

Just when I thought I was safe, I heard my name called..."Mr. Maberry, would you please come to the board and solve this problem?" I had my own problems. I didn't need his problems, too. I wanted to resist, but knew if I hesitated too long I would probably be flushed out with tear gas, or the student in front of me would get riddled with flying chalk, offering his body as a sacrifice on my behalf. So I made the long, lonely trek to the front of the class, knowing it was going to be a stare-down between me and the blackboard. I knew the blackboard would win handily, since my mind was on vacation, having left me for dead.

In between bouts with the blackboard, I tried to get a pardon. I got little sympathy.

Since Mr. Rottweiler was the vice principal, I asked him if I could take swats instead of algebra. "I would be delighted to give you several swats," he said, "but you'll still have to take algebra."

I knew I wouldn't be getting any credit for algebra, so I asked if I could get credit for the swats. "No," he said, "they wouldn't transfer to another school."

I asked him if I could get an early release. He said, "No, you have to serve your twelve weeks." I thought three weeks in algebra was enough punishment.

If I was going to see freedom, I would have to learn how to solve for x. I had enough trouble solving for Rottweiler. If I was going to solve for x, my mind and I would have to agree on a time to meet. Working together might be asking too much. But it was worth a try.

After being held captive for over twelve weeks as a **P.O.A.** (*Prisoner of Algebra*) under Mr. Rottweiler, I was beginning to think I would be spending the rest of my life chained to an algebra book.

Then the day of reckoning arrived. I was hunkered down behind my fortress, when I heard a loud, rolling, thunderous voice. I peeked over the top of my sandbags. It was Mr. Rottweiler. "Mr. Maberry, here is your report card," he announced.

It was **Judgment Day**. My very future was just inside that card. Would I be granted my release, or would I continue to wander in the xyz wilderness? My hands trembled as I slowly opened the card. Peeking inside, I almost collapsed. My grade was just enough to allow for my release.

My wandering mind had found the courage to return and solve for x. It had pulled off a coup and rescued me from algebra. It joined me for the celebration. I'm surprised it wasn't awarded the *Medal of Valor* for heroism.

As I left the room and entered the outside world, I heard bands playing and a large crowd cheering. I shook hands and held babies. My mind and I were looking forward to a summer of fun.

If there would have been a class for wandering minds, I'm sure mine would have been at the head of the class; probably receiving an award of achievement, although, I'm sure I would have had to receive the award in its absence.

News flash! I just received some good news. A recent study found one of the leading causes of poor grades to be schoolwork. I'm relieved it was schoolwork and not me. I've finally been vindicated.

The Enforcer

Recently, I was watching my granddaughter, Mallory, practice her multiplication tables. I was impressed by the fact that she suffered few ill effects from the encounter. That was not the case when I was doing hand-to-hand combat with the multiplication tables in the sixth grade.

My run-ins with math usually brought on watery eyes, shortness of breath, dizziness, incontinence, and general nausea. The fact that I escaped with most of my faculties intact should have earned me the *Distinguished Survivor Award*.

Watching my granddaughter caused me to reflect back on my own school years. How could I forget those heart-pounding, near-death experiences...*Miss Hatchet*, *Algebra*, *Biology*, and *school lunches*, to name a few.

For years my life had been completely free of such nuances. But once school began, these experiences seemed to appear with alarming frequency. They soon provided sufficient evidence that I should apply for other work. Some of my teachers applied for other work.

I quickly learned that who you had for a teacher was critical to your development. If you were a lazy, slothful, good-for-nothing slacker, you needed a teacher who could nurture those qualities; someone who could develop your laziness to its full potential. If you got a teacher who insisted that you do your work properly; who expected you to be a respectable, productive member of society, it could be a very long year. I had several years that disappeared into infinity.

I needed a teacher who could nurture my wandering mind; possibly point it in the right direction. Getting the wrong teacher would mean sucking oxygen through a straw in my underground bunker or spending the rest of the year seeking asylum in the school restroom.

After what happened to my cousin, Marky, I didn't want to find myself under the thumb of "**Olga, the Intimidator**." If I did, life would not be pretty. It would be a long year in the restroom.

Marky did not commit a grievous crime. But what he did was a serious error in judgment on his part. He wore low-hung pants to school. He thought it was "*cool*." Several students applauded. Olga was not impressed. She got a grip on Marky's pants and pulled them up so high, he was peering through his zipper and singing soprano down his pant leg. Then she fastened them in place with a safety pin. The low-hung pants were short-lived. Marky is still getting treatment for emotional duress.

With the approach of each school year, the suspense would build..."*Who will I have for a teacher?*" It was no different this particular year.

It was ten o'clock in the morning. I had been sleeping soundly, preparing for the fourth grade, when I was rudely awakened by my mother. "I talked to your new teacher this morning," she said.

"Who was that?" I asked, holding my breath in anticipation.

"Miss Hatchet," mom answered.

All my breath packed up its bags and fled out the window. I would be spending my entire year with Miss Hatchet, better known as "**The Enforcer**," a partner in scare tactics with the "Intimidator."

I remember riding my bike around town. I would pedal by Miss Hatchet's home. Viewed from a distance, she seemed like a normal person…working in the yard, sitting on the porch, reading the newspaper, smiling and waving as I passed by. But somewhere between the porch and school, she underwent a radical transformation, appearing in the classroom as **Attila the Hun**. I was certain, if I went in her basement, I would find kids from last year, chained to a desk, doing math problems.

She was a rather large, but sturdy, old maid; someone who had never married. She had dedicated her life to scaring the wits out of little kids.

As Mom escorted me to school that first day, I felt like a fourth grader being drug to slaughter. As it turned out, I just needed a couple of bandages for two skinned knees. Once the bandages were applied, I didn't think Mom would leave me. This was because I had a death grip on her leg, restricting blood flow, and almost causing her to black out. She managed to grab hold of a chair to steady herself, then shook her leg until she broke free, leaving only my hands still firmly attached to her ankle.

"Wake is a little nervous about the first day, "she said. "Do you think he will be alright?" Before I could answer the question, the Enforcer interrupted," Don't worry, Mrs. Maberry, I'll keep an eye on your son." I was just thankful it wasn't both eyes.

Quickly, I glanced out the window and saw slides, swings, and monkey bars, with kids playing and laughing. With my acute sense of discernment due, in part, to my previous years as a **P.O.W**. (*Prisoner of Washington grade school*), I realized immediately that this was probably a diversionary tactic, leading me to believe there would be time for fun. Then I spotted the paddle on her desk. It had to be the same paddle she used last school year, when she was perfecting her swing. I was sure it was still warm. She was probably letting it cool. Escaping it was my goal. If I succeeded, I might receive the award for "*Outstanding Achievement.*"

As other kids started filing in, I began getting insider information. I would have to wait until recess to get outsider information.

"My dad said I'd better behave for Miss Hatchet because she rules with an iron hand," Donny informed us.

"Wow, I've never seen anyone with an iron hand," said Jimmy.

"Neither have I," Billy chimed in. "Maybe she'll let me borrow it for show and tell."

"I'm sure we'll all get to see it," I said, nervously looking over my shoulder.

I didn't know why Miss Hatchet needed an iron hand. She already had a paddle.

Hanging up our coats in the cloakroom, we could hear faint scratching inside the wall and wondered if it was a student from last year, who hadn't completed his work.

Reading, writing, and math were Miss Hatchet's priorities. Having spent considerable time with Gramps, I thought she should be instructing us in how to parch peanuts, thump a watermelon, and how to make homemade ice cream. She wasn't interested in my priorities. According to the Enforcer, my sole purpose in fourth grade was to read, write, and figure out numbers. It was obviously more than I could handle. School stretched far into eternity that year.

If Miss Hatchet left the room, no one moved, because she had a nasty habit of appearing without notice. If you got out of your seat while she was out of the room, she would appear like she had just slipped under the door. We never could figure out how she got the iron hand under the door, but there it was, looming over us. You had to duck when she walked by, so the hand wouldn't hit you in the head and knock you unconscious. It silenced any talk of mutiny.

Miss Hatchet had one student who was the apple of her eye. No, it wasn't me. I was math bait. She would feed me to the blackboard, where math problems would suck the life out of me.

I tried to stay out of her sight by sitting behind the biggest student in class, but The Enforcer would hear the beads of perspiration dripping from my forehead and splashing on the floor, creating a small pool. "Mr. Maberry," she would say sternly, "would you please come to the board." I would remove myself from inside the student's shirt in front of me and slither to the front of the class.

I always dreamed of reciting a sports score or sharing some fascinating weather trivia, but dreams never came true in Miss Hatchet's class…just math problems that always seemed to need immediate attention.

"Mr. Maberry, would you please work this problem?" asked Miss Hatchet, barely able to conceal her joy, as my legs quivered, and my hands fumbled with the chalk. I stared at the problem. It stared at me, refusing to leave the board. Everyone's attention was riveted on me as they waited for an answer. I hated the riveting, but I had no answer.

While they waited, I prayed for an *earthquake, flooding, appendicitis, kidney stones*…anything to avoid the menacing glare of the problem waiting restlessly to be solved. If I waited much longer, I was certain it would start pacing back and forth, across the front of the board.

Glancing at Miss Hatchet, I knew I didn't have much time left. I had to make a move. I remembered the advice of an old math sage, or maybe it was Sally, sitting in the desk behind me…*"If you don't know the answer, guess. You always have a chance of being right."* So I guessed. Then I heard a voice in the math wilderness saying, *"**Very good, Mr. Maberry.**"* It was the voice of The Enforcer. I had guessed correctly. Overcome with emotion, I grabbed a desk to steady myself. Everyone cheered. I felt like a hero. I had gone to the blackboard and conquered the enemy…a testy math problem. Returning to my desk, I hunkered down, and waited for my next confrontation with numbers.

I have no idea where Miss Hatchet went to school to become a teacher, but I'm certain she specialized in *"hovering."* She was always looking over your shoulder to see how your work was coming along. This is probably why she was always telling me to sit up in my seat. I would sit so low, trying to avoid her, she couldn't find my shoulders. She would just stop and stare at the small mass in my chair. "Is that you, Mr. Maberry?"

"Yes, Miss Hatchet."

"Well, you need to sit up, so I can look over your shoulder."

"Yes, Miss Hatchet."

Between her iron hand and hovering, she was an overpowering presence.

At night, when I was asleep, I would dream of her hovering over me, holding dripping, wet math papers she had rescued from the irrigation ditch, where they had gone on a joy ride. "Mr. Maberry, look what I found, with your name on them." I would bolt upright, with my heart in my mouth. "I'm sorry Miss Hatchet! They must have slipped out of my notebook when I was walking by the ditch. Next time I will be more careful." *Then I would awaken* to the terrible taste of heart-in-mouth, realizing it was just a horrible nightmare.

"Is your work done, Mr. Maberry?" I don't know why Miss Hatchet asked such a silly question. Mine was always a work in progress, much like your tax dollars at work. She expected me to have my schoolwork completed by the end of the day. The problem was our differing views on the definition of *"the end of the day"*. Miss Hatchet's "end of day" was the school dismissal bell. Mine was anytime beyond bedtime. Her day didn't allow me enough time to complete my work. My day would have allowed enough time if I would have remembered it before the next morning.

To strengthen my memory skills, Miss Hatchet would keep me after school, and use me for sport with math problems. "Try this one…try that one…here's a nice problem…and on it went. After several sessions, I became restless and decided it was time for a break, as in daring escape. I waited until she walked the school bus kids out to their bus. As soon as she went out the back door, I shot out the front door, completely ignoring the possibility of finding my picture tacked to a utility pole, with a sizeable bounty on my head. I ran like the wind for home. Actually, I think I passed the wind along the way. Arriving home, I ran inside and quickly slammed the door, making sure to push the couch in front of it, in case the Enforcer tried to break it down. All of a sudden she appeared, like an apparition, hovering at the door, motioning for me to come out. I closed my eyes, and then opened them again, to see if the apparition was real. It was. I figured I might as well save the door, and walk out under my own power.

47

Getting into her car, I said, "I don't think Mom would want me riding alone, with a young lady. (I was hoping flattery would save my life.)

"I agree with your Mom," answered Miss Hatchet. "But I'm an old maid, and I'm your teacher. I don't think she will care if you ride back to school with me to finish those math problems that are patiently waiting to be solved."

I questioned whether I could survive this overpowering presence until the end of the year. To your good fortune, I survived.

After a year with Miss Hatchet, summer never looked sweeter. Skies were bluer, the birds chirped louder, the days were longer, there were no assignments to complete, and my wandering mind had rejoined me for a summer of fun. It was a wonderful time to be alive.

Years later, when I became a teacher, and my students had wandering minds and difficulty completing assignments, my time in The Enforcer's class had prepared me for it. I just hope kids didn't hear the scratching inside the wall in the cloakroom.

Learning Hard Work

Like many young people, I was fascinated with magic tricks during my youth. I was hoping to learn enough to make algebra disappear or, at least, turn my teacher, Mr. Rottweiler, into a beautiful princess. (If I could have accomplished the latter, I may have attempted calculus and physics.) The only thing I made disappear was a nice coat I had gotten for Christmas. It was one of my more expensive acts.

I also had an interest in the Arts. I was especially fond of the **Art of Escape**. Watching Houdini free himself, after being bound in chains, was very impressive. Even more impressive was watching someone free themselves from algebra.

Gramps wasn't impressed. "My stars, anybody can do that," he said. "I think you're a far better escape artist, the way you can escape hard work. How do you do it?"

"It's a secret, Gramps. If I shared it with everyone, there would be no one left to do hard work."

"*Goooood Gracious*, I don't know about that boy," Gramps muttered to himself, as he walked away.

Gramps had taught his children the value of hard work and he tried to impress it upon me, although I wasn't all that impressed.

Having learned hard work as a child growing up in Alabama, Mom loved sharing her experiences with me. "When I was your age I was picking cotton all day in the hot sun, while watching for poisonous snakes," she'd ramble on. She wanted me to experience that same joy. But I was perfectly content pulling the covers over my head, and going back to sleep. Besides, there was no cotton or poisonous snakes where we lived. That was fine with me, because I didn't think I could pick cotton and watch for poisonous snakes at the same time. My time would have been devoted to snake patrol.

Gramps was concerned about my lifestyle as a *"budding"* slacker. Fearing that I might fall prey to *"easy money,"* to supplement my lifestyle, he warned me about get-rich-quick schemes. I reassured him that I wasn't going to Alabama to pick cotton. Poisonous snakes that enjoy leg of cotton picker weren't worth the money.

A short time later, hard work called. I was offered a job *"bucking hay."* This meant picking up hay bales twice my size and throwing them onto the bed of a speeding truck. I was ready to take the job, but in a dream the night before, I was warned it was a get-rich-quick scheme, and that I should flee to South America. With no car, I would have to flee on foot. With no money, the closest I could get to South America was the south side of our house, where I had my secret underground bunker.

I wasn't sure how long I would be able to hide there, since it was a well-known secret. But the location was perfect. It was on a major supply route...the bunker to the refrigerator. Hopefully, I would be able to hang on until I was offered something more legitimate.

With all my friends involved in hard work, and other suspicious activities, I decided to focus on developing my mind. After all, my teachers said it was one of the most undeveloped regions of the world.

I was particularly interested in the field of statistical analysis. Each day I would scour the sports pages, as well as the weather page, gathering critical information that was basically useless trivia. But for those who loved useless trivia, it was very useful.

I would always try to share my storehouse of knowledge with my cousin, Lester. But fearing a withering attack of sports scores and weather facts, he would just run home, lock himself in his room, and put a Land Shark (often referred to as a Chihuahua) on guard. He had no interest in who won an important ballgame, or how many degrees the temperature rose during a two-minute period in Spearfish, South Dakota, in 1943---(On January 22, 1943, the temperature went from four below zero to forty-five above zero in two minutes; a world record.)

With my knowledge in useless information, I was certain I would land a job with a major sports team, or the national weather service.

While I was waiting for my dream offer, a scout for the local news service called and offered me a not-so-lucrative, long-term contract as a paperboy. Being concerned about my image as a slacker, I was skeptical. But Mom encouraged me to take the job. She said it would be far better than spending the rest of my life as an orphan.

My new venture gave me the opportunity to develop my throwing arm for baseball by riding around town on my bike, throwing newspapers onto people's porches. Only once did a paper take a bad bounce and end up in a customer's living room. The next day I took a bad bounce and ended up in their living room...with money for the broken window.

During the winter, I lost some of my enthusiasm for throwing newspapers. That was probably because it's hard to throw newspapers when your hands are numb. I checked my long-term contract to see if it included winter delivery. It did. Then I checked to see if there was an "escape clause." There was none. I dreamed of a paper route in Florida. After learning I would have to hitchhike 3000 miles and sleep on the street, the dream lost its appeal. I blew more hot air on my hands, and rolled another newspaper.

The winter was getting longer. I considered firing my agent, but I didn't like the prospect of being homeless. As the winter cold wore on, I collected my toes and fingers and saved them in a box until they could be re-attached in the spring.

After that first winter, I wanted out of my contract, but my agent said something to the affect that "if you don't work, you don't eat." I knew I would miss eating, so I kept throwing newspapers.

After years of hardship, my long-term contract as a paperboy expired. I now had more time to try and corral my wandering mind, as it vacationed at will, stopping occasionally to assist me in the classroom.

One day I found myself graduating from high school. I have no idea how I found myself there. Even my teachers were surprised. "Wow, I can't believe you're here," they said.

"I agree," I answered. "It's one of the great unsolved mysteries of my time."

Gramps said my graduating from high school was one of the greatest escape acts he had ever witnessed; almost as good as my escape from hard work.

Impressed with my ability to escape hard work, and then make a diploma magically appear, I set my sights on college.

While in college, one of my instructors caught me by surprise... "Mr. Maberry, "he said, "Why don't you become a teacher? You would be great!"

"Is this a get-rich-quick scheme?" I asked.

"Definitely not," he insisted. "In fact, you'll probably have to get a second job."

"I'd prefer a get-rich-quick scheme."

"Have you thought about running for Congress?"

I was too young for Congress. So I turned my attention to education instead...far, far away from the "*easy money*."

Once in the classroom, I found myself ensnared in a life of hard work; a shadow of my former self. I could hardly face myself in the mirror.

After toiling for years in education, and barely escaping with my life, I joined E.A. (Educator's Anonymous); a support group for recovering educators.

I had almost recovered from those years of hard work, when Lester approached me about writing this book. "Is this another get-rich-quick scheme?" I asked.

"No, no," said Lester. "You probably won't even make a dime."

"That's more than I'm making now. I think I'll try it."

Lester is pleased that I've written the book. And Gramps would be proud. I've learned hard work.

A Plan Gone Astray

Plans are good. They keep you tracking in the right direction.
But sometimes they don't work. So you have to be prepared with a
backup plan. I like to call it Plan B, or C, or D, depending on how
many backup plans you need. My teachers exhausted the entire
alphabet trying to find the right plan for me. "Have you tried Plan
Z?" my counselor asked one of my teacher's.

I love having a good plan, but I've discovered life is much more
adventuresome without one. And plans can go astray; just wander
off. I, personally, have had grand plans that have done this very
thing; like mowing the lawn. I told my wife I had planned to mow it,
but the plan wandered off. I looked everywhere. I had to resort to
Plan B...the golf course. After eighteen holes, I found my original
plan relaxing and joking with the guys in the clubhouse. With some
vigorous coaxing, I managed to talk it into mowing the lawn.

Just yesterday my five year old grandson was getting into my car. "Grandpa," he said, "you need to clean out your car."

"I had planned on doing that this morning, Braxten, but my plan went astray," I answered, feigning control of the discussion.

"What's 'astray'," Grandpa?"

"I'm glad you asked. Now listen carefully. This could happen to you someday. Just as I was going to clean the car, my mind was attracted to something that was far more exciting, so it wandered off in another direction; in other words, it went "astray.""

"Oh. Did it go to the coffee shop, Grandpa?"

"I'm too old to remember the fine details, Braxten, but wherever it went, it caused me to forget about cleaning the car."

"Oh?"

I don't know why my wife can't understand such a simple explanation.

During the Dark Ages, I thought I had the perfect plan for my life; *climbing cherry trees, playing in irrigation ditches,* and *running wild and free* on Gramps' Ranch. There was no rush for school. I could begin when I was ready; around the age of forty.

But there were others who felt there was more to life than this. If there was, I hadn't heard about it. Surely there wasn't more to life than running wild and free.

They told me there was a big world out there, and their plan was to prepare me for it. I couldn't imagine a world bigger than my own. I thought my world was just the right size. I was perfectly content with cherry trees and irrigation ditches.

"No, no," they said, "you need reading, writing, math, woodshop, algebra, biology, band and anything else we think will prepare you for a big, new world." They really didn't mention all those subjects, but that's what they meant.

My life was about to take a new direction. **SCHOOL**! It cut sharply into my wild and free time. It would also prove to be the biggest obstacle in my path to graduation. I asked if there was a backup plan.

My experiment with school went smoothly in the beginning, probably because the life of a lab rat had always been appealing to me. I enjoyed playing with the giant blocks and lying on the rug listening to stories, and taking naps. Then some undercover kindergartener was tipped off by his older brother that it wouldn't be this way through high school. In fact, it wouldn't be this way next year. I could see life coming to an end.

I wanted to repeat kindergarten. But after graduating with honors in *"Advanced Napping,"* my teacher said I had to move on to greater challenges.

With no building blocks and naps, I would be facing the greatest challenge of my life. I could see problems on the horizon.

I must have gotten too close to the horizon because one of my problems was standing beside me. It was Mrs. Haller, the elementary school principal. She introduced me to the school paddle. Years later, the school was re-named *Helen Haller Middle School*, in her honor. I don't know if she earned the honor because she had given me a swat, or she earned it on her own merit. Nevertheless, if I had known I was getting a swat from a famous person, I would have asked for a signed paddle; probably even asked for more swats. I don't recollect the reason for the swat, but there didn't have to be much reason in those days. I think mine was for floating schoolwork in the irrigation ditch. I loved watching schoolwork bob up and down in the water until it capsized and went under. I thought that was far more fun than watching the carefully crafted model boat I had been working on for three months, drift downstream and out of sight, never to be seen again.

School may have been more enticing if there had been a row of cherry trees in the hall, or an irrigation ditch running through the middle of the classroom, but just sitting behind a desk was more than I could handle. So my mind would wander off to cherry trees, irrigation ditches, and backup plans. It sorely missed the wild and free life that was calling outside the classroom. With each passing day, it was spending less time in school, and more time enjoying getaways. I called it *"Wandering Mind"* Travel.

While most of my classmates took the expressway to graduation, I took a different road. It was like a winding, one lane logging road with deep ruts and numerous switchbacks. It appeared there had been several washouts. The road was almost impassable. Just when I thought I would get through, I would be stopped by a roadblock...*math, band, woodshop, biology,* or some other immovable obstacle. Who knew when I would arrive at graduation?

If third grade was any indication, it would be a late arrival. **Miss Hognose** had divided our class into reading groups. Each group was named after a species of bird. First were the *Bluebirds*. They were the best readers. I wasn't in that group. Following the Bluebirds were the *Robins*; another miss. Next were the *Chickadees*; missed again. I could see a pattern developing. I was hoping to land somewhere before Miss Hognose ran out of birds. Then I heard my name..."Mr. Maberry, you're with the *Dying Quails*." I felt like I had just been shot out of the sky. It was a hard landing. I could hear the dogs barking. I think they were called off by Miss Hognose.

She informed us that we would be reading the **Life** and **Times** of **Dick and Jane**. Hoping to avoid becoming road kill, and survive the third grade, I did my best to learn about these kids. Their lives seemed to be dedicated to running, skipping, and jumping. We took turns reading aloud in our groups..."See Dick. See Dick run. Run, Dick, run. See Dick stop to catch his breath. Let's see Jane while Dick catches his breath. See Jane skip. Skip, Jane, skip. Oh, oh! Jane fell. Sorry Jane. There's Spot, their dog. See Spot. See Spot jump. Down, Spot, down. See Spot chase the mailman. See Spot get pepper-sprayed. See the mailman chase Spot."

After nine months of Dick and Jane, I could see fourth grade in the distance. The *Dying Quail* was still flapping.

Years later, I found myself stalled in the sixth grade. I had been ambushed by the multiplication tables.

I figured someone would rescue me and send me back to where I belonged...climbing cherry trees and running wild and free on Gramps' ranch. Couldn't they see I wasn't ready for school? Instead, I was left at the disposal of one Mr. Sanford. He was actually a kindly man, with a strange name, who was determined to keep me moving through school. To keep moving, I would have to sharpen my recollection of the multiplication tables. He said I had to know them better if I was going to move on to *"higher learning."* I thought sixth grade was "higher learning." I was badly mistaken.

Mr. Sanford arranged for me to meet the multiplication tables after school. It sounded like poor scheduling to me, but he didn't seem to mind staying late into the night and coming in every day during the summer, including weekends and holidays, and missing that vacation he and his wife had been planning for years.

By the end of the following summer, I had gotten to know the multiplication tables extremely well. With Mr. Sanford's approval, along with a sigh of relief, I was granted a pardon from sixth grade.

Summer vacation was short-lived that year. I put in a request for an extension, but it was denied.

With little time to prepare, I was on my way to higher learning. **Junior High**! My road narrowed to a foot path. I found it difficult getting through. It began with seventh grade band. Mom wanted me to have some culture, and band was the perfect class to get *"cultured."* I would be playing the trumpet, the instrument of her choice. It was an adjustment, from reading books to reading notes.

I soon learned that first chair in the trumpet section was the lead trumpet. This meant you were better than everyone else. They don't tell you that, but it's true. After first chair, was second chair, third chair, and on down to last chair. Last chair means your Mom signed you up for the wrong class. Not wanting to be last, I pulled my shiny, new trumpet out of its case and began practicing for first chair. "I may have signed you up for the wrong class," said Mom.

The time finally came for chair assignments.

"Let me hear what you can play," said my instructor, **Mr. Bonefetcher.**

After listening, he recommended the electric chair, but said he would be open to lethal injection.

Despite his recommendation, I remained in the band. I loved his sense of humor.

I did my best, but reality has a harsh way of exacting cruel vengeance. Mr. Bonefetcher assigned me to sixth chair. It was particularly disheartening, considering there were only five chairs.

But each week, I had the opportunity to vindicate myself. I could choose a piece of music, and challenge the person in front of me. If I won the competition, I could move up a chair. On the pre-arranged day, we would be sent to the sound room. Each of us would play my chosen musical piece. Then the rest of the class would vote on No. 1 or No. 2. The winner would be flown to Disneyland for three days. *Just kidding*! If I won, I would move up a chair, and flaunt my haughty position. If I lost, it would be another thorn in my hat.

I challenged numerous times, and ended up with a hat full of thorns. Mr. Bonefetcher said playing the scale really couldn't be considered a musical piece.

With little effort, I was able to convince everyone within ear range that music wasn't in my future. They were hoping my music wasn't in their future, either.

I decided to skip band my senior year. Mom finally agreed; my classmates had gone through enough suffering. Music wasn't the plan for my future. It was a nice idea, but it was a plan gone astray.

Mr. Bonefetcher hid his disappointment behind a big smile.

In high school, biology stood in my path to graduation. I wanted to take another path, but it was blocked by woodshop. Every path was blocked. I would have to get through biology.

The time I had spent bonding with the frogs at the lake on Gramps' ranch, may have prepared me for biology, but it didn't prepare me for **Mrs. Stonecold**.

She was a stern taskmaster with a large collection of frogs, all peering at me through a jar. The "**Jar**" was their fate. There was no escape. Besides, they were dead.

This was a time when frogs had very few rights. It was a time when I had very few rights.

In Mrs. Stonecold's class, frogs didn't get respect; they got dissected.

She was determined to teach our class how to perform a dissection.

I wasn't interested in amphibian juice. So I would test her determination.

Besides, these may have been the frogs I had spent time with at the lake; frogs that had competed in the frog hopping contests as part of the annual *Leapfrog Games*.

I felt sorry for the frogs; from a home on the lake, to a jar on the teacher's desk. Frankly, if I had been a frog, and knew my family and friends were being hauled off to the "*Jar*", and then dissected in high school biology labs, I would have abandoned my lakefront home, and looked for a good frog support group in town, or joined the frog underground.

Sitting in the back of the class--where most critical thinkers sit--I contemplated the fate of the frogs. Mrs. Stonecold said I was daydreaming. I called it contemplating. It had more substance, and made me appear to be more than a slacker.

The *Day of Dissection* finally arrived. Even though I had no formal training as a frog surgeon, Mrs. Stonecold would not accept my incompetence as a reason to avoid surgery.

I was reluctant to display my cutlery skills, especially on frogs I may have known at the lake. Mrs. Stonecold didn't share my sentiments. She was more interested in me learning to dissect a frog.

Shortly after she began her lesson on dissection, I became involved in an *Advanced Contemplating* session. I wondered if it was too late to donate Mr. Froggy's legs to a local restaurant. As I continued to contemplate this matter, I set Mr. Froggy on the open window ledge, next to my desk. Moments later, everyone heard a scream. I looked for Mr. Froggy, but he was missing. I quickly connected the dots: *Missing frog + scream* = **TROUBLE**! Since our class was on the second floor, everyone ran to the windows and looked down. There was Miss Buttonwillow, waving her arms wildly, and dancing and twirling around like a top. She had been walking below, near the building, when she was suddenly attacked by a flying frog...or so the story went. Mr. Froggy was found in the rose beds, resting peacefully.

It was a great show for a moment in time; until I was rudely awakened by Mrs. Stonecold throwing cold water on my dream. "Mr. Maberry, may I have your attention?" I must have fallen asleep during her inspirational lecture on the dissection of a frog.

It didn't look good for me as I made the trek to the principal's office. I feared I could be spending the rest of the quarter peering through a jar on Mrs. Stonecold's desk.

After a short discussion with the principal, I returned to class. I had escaped the "**Jar!**"

I'm not sure how I escaped biology. But I knew it would be some time before Mrs. Stonecold recovered.

My teachers had grand plans for my future. But those plans had wandered off. They didn't want to be associated with me. They may have succeeded if I could have sat in a cherry tree in class, rather than behind a desk. While their plans had gone astray, I waited patiently to try my plan.

I had learned everything I needed to know in life from Gramps. I had frequented coffee shops, golf courses, ballgames, and traveled around the state. After spending years under Gramps' tutelage, I had mapped out my future. I knew where I was going. Some thought it was politics, but I had a better plan.

I was nearing my last breath on the hamster wheel, when I received the call to meet with my career guidance counselor. Together we would map out my field of study for the future. I knew I wasn't going to choose a field with a bull in it.

Most of my classmates wanted to go into education, medicine, foreign languages, or some other menial endeavor. I had other ideas.

"So, Mr. Maberry, what field have you chosen for your future?" asked my counselor.

"I'd like to go into Retirement," I answered.

"Retirement?" he questioned, briefly stunned.

"That's right," I answered. "I understand retirement."

Being around Gramps, I felt I knew everything there was to know about retirement. I could converse with anyone over coffee. I had learned key words, such as Hawaii, Caribbean, tee time, and

Certificate of Deposit. I had even won "Best of Show" at the county fair for my pill box display. I couldn't drive like Gramps, but I could pick up those skills at a stunt-driving school.

I liked what I saw in retirement. I knew it was something I could do.

Then my counselor said something that shook the pillars of my big new world…"You'll have to work before going into retirement," he said.

"When can I opt out of work," I answered.

"When you're ready to retire," he continued.

"I'm ready now!"

"You haven't worked!"

"The timing isn't right!"

Things were getting complicated. I re-considered the field with a bull in it.

"Do you have another plan?" asked my counselor. "Is there something else you would enjoy…something where you might achieve greatness?"

"Well, maybe Assisted Living. Mom says I've been in it for the past seventeen years, and I've excelled beyond her wildest expectations."

There was silence. I heard a feather hit the floor.

Pulling himself together, my counselor asked, "Has work ever entered your mind?"

"Only as a last option," I answered.

Needing money for room and board, I finally decided on the last option. Work! Then I discovered that work is the primary cause of aging.

Why didn't they prepare me for this in the fourth grade?

I hope I live long enough to enjoy my plan. I hope it's not a plan gone astray.

Gridiron Martyrs

Like many young boys, I loved sports. I enjoyed the competition, and it relieved the pain of schoolwork.

Baseball was my favorite sport. I also enjoyed basketball. But I took a more cautious approach to football. I played one year; in the ninth grade. I considered playing in high school, but common sense prevailed.

I put a high value on life after school. According to the player's practicing under Coach Hardman, life didn't exist after school, as I knew it.

Coach Hardman's conditioning drills were legendary. Players ran laps until sunset. I thought walking between classes was enough conditioning. After some unidentified players put several geese in his car one night, the legend exploded. Rumors began flying around the school about Coach Hardman's drills..."Watch out! Another rumor is coming in for a landing." I wondered who would be the first martyr. I was thankful for my momentary lapse into common sense.

Still, Coach Hardman managed to round up just enough players to field a football team; players that were willing to sacrifice their well-being for gridiron martyrdom.

Several blocks from my childhood home, someone recently unearthed an old tattered jersey, some shoulder pads with the pads missing, along with several rusty cleats from an old pair of football shoes.

Some of the native townspeople were called in to explain these findings. What they discovered were ancient football burial grounds dating back to the early 1960's. The site was once called the *"greenfield,"* a field where kids in town would go to play football on Saturdays during football season.

I still remember getting those phone calls. "Hey, Maberry, wanna go play some football; maybe chip a few teeth or dislocate a shoulder?"

"Great!" I'd say. "See you there in a few minutes."

The *"greenfield"* was also where our high school played their football games. It was a field without lights. This is probably why we played day games. After we got lights, we played our games at night. There were some who thought we should play our night games without lights. They felt we would win more games in the dark.

It was on this very field that our football team would go down in infamy; flames, too, but especially infamy. I'm surprised no one questioned why we had a football team. After all, we won only one game in three years, and it's still under investigation.

It was the ninth grade. "Maberry, why don't you turn out for football?" Charlie asked.

"I'm definitely playing this year," I heard someone say. Then I realized the voice had come from me. By the time I had walked home from school, I was black and blue from hitting myself for such a poor decision. I had my entire life in front of me. Now I could see it in the rear view mirror. There was an aid car with sirens and flashing lights! It didn't look good. I considered changing my mind, but commitments were not taken lightly in the ninth grade. Failing to follow through on my ill-advised decision would label me a black sheep; a fate far worse than treason. Football would be life on the edge. I just had to remind myself not to look over the edge.

The day for issuing uniforms came so quickly, I didn't have time to plan an escape. I watched expectantly as the coach handed everyone their gold pants, pads, and shiny gold helmet. When it was my turn, he handed me my gold pants, pads, and then said, "Maberry, we don't have any more gold helmets. You'll have to wear this white helmet."

"*Wow! I wonder if anyone will notice me,*" I thought to myself. I felt like a white rat in a lab experiment. I was already too close to the edge. I looked down to see if I could survive the jump. The black sheep began to look appealing. I should have been penalized fifteen yards with a loss of down for such a poor decision, but I decided I would continue with the experiment.

After three weeks of turf n' mouth, that fateful day arrived; game day. My number was 32. I played end, which meant I was on the end of the line. *This is great*, I thought, *the opposing team will never notice me.* I was sadly mistaken. During warm-ups, I quickly caught their attention. "Look," they yelled, "a white helmet!"

It was soon game time. I barely had enough time to get my spot on the bench warm when coach gave the call. "Maberry, come here."

"Yes, Coach?"

"Let's run a 32 end around. Now get in there."

I ran into the huddle. "32 end around," I barked. Then I looked across at the opposing line and my life flashed before my eyes. I dreamed of one day growing up and having a family, but I knew that one step across the line of scrimmage and all those plans could change.

As everyone broke from the huddle, I broke for the sidelines. I noticed all the players were waving as I was nearing the coach. It looked as though they were waving for me to come back, but that couldn't be, I thought. I'd just been in.

"Why are you back?" asked the coach. "You were supposed to stay in. The play was going to you."

For whatever reason, I didn't know this rule..."when you take a play into the huddle, you stay in...period." It must have been providential. I now had more time to think about my future. And it looked much brighter.

As soon as I realized the direction my life was taking, fertilizer for the football field, I came to my senses. Knowing I might want to write a book one day, I chose to be an observer the next three years. I watched everyone else become fertilizer.

I would love to see a town memorial honoring all those who gave blood, sweat, teeth and tears during those three years. They've never truly been recognized, not even their name and picture on a bag of *"Weed and Feed."* I've heard talk of a movie being made to commemorate those years. It's called *Friday Night Lights Out.* It has an R rating for gratuitous violence. If you allow your children to see it, I recommend they wear a blindfold.

Note: Coach Hardman would probably tell you that football was a hard sell in our town. And it was! We were a small school. Most of our games were played against much larger schools. As hard as our teams fought, scores would often be lop-sided. This was especially true of our arch nemesis, the school where John Elway's father once coached.

They were fifteen miles to our west. I have no idea why we were on their schedule. It was no rival. They came from a city of 15,000. We came from a dairy town of 1000, where cows ruled. It was an uneven playing field, favoring our arch rival. We might have leveled the field if cows could have suited up. We could've put them on the offensive line.

A gale force wind was blowing when our nemesis arrived for our Friday night game. They had come to make us their annual sacrifice to the football gods. (I hated the football gods. I wondered who, on their board, was responsible for pitting us against these gorillas.) Anyway, it wasn't long before we heard a rolling thunder and felt the ground shake as players were herded by our locker room on the way to the playing field. "If they think that stuff is going to intimidate us, they're doing a good job," said Clifford.

It was their names that caught everyone's attention: names like *Igor, Hulk, Troll, Fang, Crusher,* and *John.* Their fullback, Hulk, looked like a boxcar with legs. When he ran, everyone stepped back and watched. Hulk didn't appear to have a neck; just a head between his collarbone.

They had 60 players in uniform, standing along the sidelines, arms at their side, knuckles dragging the ground. We had sixteen players in uniform, nowhere to be found. They were discovered in the locker room with the door locked and lights out.

To get them out, coach Hardman appealed to their sense of pride. They moved deeper into the locker room. He would have to try another tactic...a week off from school in return for playing against these giant alien creatures from a far-off school district. The players ran out on the field for pre-game warm-ups.

After the warm-ups, the captains of each school met at the center of the field for the coin toss. We won the toss, so we had the choice: kickoff, and let them have the ball first, or receive. We didn't like either choice.

The storm worsened as the referee's waited for our decision. "Could we mail in our answer?" asked Billy, shouting over the wind. The officials detected this as a stall tactic. They refused our request. There would be no stay of execution. We decided to receive.

Our rival kicked off into the punishing wind. The ball did not get far before it blew back onto their side of the field. Donny fell on it at their 45 yard line. It was unfamiliar territory. No one could remember the last time we had been this close to their goal line. Breaking out of the huddle, we lined up for our first play. Steve, our quarterback, looked at their defense. Apparently he didn't like what he saw because he called time out and ran to the sidelines. The rest of the team didn't like what they saw either, so everyone ran to the sidelines.

After discussing several plays, including one that would take us across the mountains and to the ocean, where we would board a passing ship, Coach sent everyone back out onto the field.

Just beyond the line of scrimmage was eternity.

Everyone lined up and stared into eternity. "There goes the ship," said one of our linemen.

Our arch rival tried some well-worn intimidation tactics. "Are you an organ donor? Do you give blood? We're taking it tonight." Their tactics worked beautifully. We considered appeasing them with ground chuck, but chuck was out with a sprained ankle.

Instead, we sent Mikey, our fullback, up the middle. He disappeared into eternity. A moment later we saw him sprinting down the sideline without the football.

Mikey returned to the bench, panting heavily. As he explained to Coach Hardman, there was a terrific pounding in his ears. It was so intense it caused him to drop the football. When he dropped the ball, to his surprise, the pounding stopped. The pounding footsteps had fallen on the loose ball. Our rival had recovered.

On their first play, they handed the ball to Hulk. He bulled through the line, bowling over, and shaking off tacklers as he roared into the secondary like a runaway locomotive. Gary was determined to make the tackle, and stop Hulk from scoring. It was evident that Gary had left his common sense at home in a drawer. He didn't have a good angle on the Hulk. It was going to be a head-on collision. Everyone in the crowd held their breath, as they fixed their eyes on the coming wreck. I couldn't watch. I closed my eyes and listened for impact. When I didn't hear the sound of someone being steamrolled into a decal for the football field, I looked up. Gary had slipped and fallen, missing his chance for martyrdom. A sigh of relief rolled through the crowd. The driver of the aid car turned off the engine. Hulk rumbled in for the touchdown.

We kicked off to start the second half. With a horrific wind at our backs, the kickoff landed somewhere in the next county. A new ball was brought in. On the first play from scrimmage, their quarterback fumbled the exchange from center. One of our linemen fell on the ball. Coach called a timeout. "Okay, guys, I'm not going to risk anymore injuries in this weather. I'm going to try the 'surprise' element. We're going to run the '*fainting goat*.'"

"Goat...? What goat? Why are we running a goat?" asked Donny. "I think Mikey is a better runner...well, at least as good as the goat."

"No, no," said Coach Hardman. "The **play** is called 'The *fainting goat.*' When Steve says, 'Hike,' everyone drops to the ground, like they've fainted. Nobody gets hurt."

"What about the goat?" Donny asked.

"Just go out there and line up like we always do. When everyone else falls to the ground, you fall to the ground. Got it?"

"I think I've got it!"

Everyone ran back onto the playing field. Just as Steve was calling the play, the lights flickered and went out. While everyone was dropping to the ground, Steve took the ball and ran for the goal line. He would have scored, but the referees had called the game. It was truly "*Friday Night Lights Out.*"

Everyone had survived our arch rival, and the windstorm of the century. There had been only minor injuries. But there would always be next year, when the gridiron martyrs, once again, faced their nemesis; those giant, alien creatures from a far-off school district...15 miles to our west.

Happy Campers

Over the years, I've often heard people called "*Happy Campers*," like "He's a happy camper." I decided to do some extensive research on the subject. After several minutes, I learned it came from being "*satisfied*" or "*content*." That made sense. As a young boy, I was always "*content*" if I could survive a night in the backyard, without being abducted by an upperclassman. I was a happy camper!

Not long ago, my wife and I attended an RV show with some friends. I immediately saw why there has been such an increase in happy campers. They're living in forty feet of luxury-on-wheels, parked in a five-star resort in a sun-drenched oasis. They're also enjoying all the amenities I'm dreaming about in the new game, "**Fantasy Retirement**": *pool, golf, shuffleboard, spas,* and roaming those *pesky flea markets.*

For those who can't afford the RV lifestyle, happy camping is still within your reach. There is now something called "**glamping**." **Glamping** is a blend of glamour and camping, with a heavy emphasis on glamour. When you're glamping, you sleep in a luxurious tent with carpet, a fireplace, TV, and fine food. Even the mosquitoes are high end. They never land on you. They just fly by and wave, like a mosquito pageant.

Okay, I'll admit, the mosquitoes are the same mosquitoes that will suck you dry, and then throw your body over a cliff. But the rest is true! I'm not making it up.

Unable to afford forty feet of luxury on wheels, or glamping, I had to resign myself to spending the remainder of my camping years in the same fashion I had spent my previous camping years; shivering in a sleeping bag, on a pile of sharp rocks and pine needles. Of course, my wife had to remind me that I wouldn't be so miserable if I would take the sharp rocks and pine needles out of my bag.

As a boy, I loved the lure of the great outdoors, especially if there were bedrooms to clean or homework to complete. There were several of us who spent many nights camping in backyards and vacant lots close to home, in case we heard rustling in the night, and suspected high school seniors nearby, who were especially skilled at rustling up underclassmen and using them for fish bait.

Sprinting at cheetah-like speed, dodging in between parked cars, jumping six-foot fences, and standing for long periods of time, disguised as shrubbery, was crucial for survival.

Everyone who camped had to be fleet afoot. If you didn't make it to the house of refuge, you could be nabbed by an upperclassman and never seen again. And you would never be a happy camper as fish food.

Having survived numerous raids, I've learned several very important truths to becoming a happy camper. First, you can't let classified information, such as your camping plans, leak out during school. This is a magnet for upperclassmen. Next, you need to have a secure campsite. This can be done by digging a moat around your camp, and stocking it with alligators. If there are no alligators, you'll have to find something else for your moat, preferably something that likes to dine on upperclassmen. Or you can line your moat with teachers handing out homework assignments. This should secure your campsite.

An absolute necessity for camping is a campfire. There is no reason to camp if you're not going to have a campfire. And I mean a reasonable campfire; not backdraft two. This means you must know how to build a campfire. A safe location is of the utmost importance. A barn full of hay is not a safe location. If you try this, you won't be a happy camper. And you may have to apply for asylum in a foreign country, such as California.

It's also important that you be in control of your fire. This means you should build your fire next to a fire truck. Being in control is critical to your well-being, along with the well-being of those around you, including all the animals in the forest.

Finally, after you have learned how to control a campfire, you must learn how to tame the smoke. This may be more difficult than controlling the fire. Personally, I've found taming the smoke more difficult than taming a homicidal rooster.

Smoke attacks me like a hungry lioness. It gets an adrenaline rush if it finds me sitting anywhere near a campfire. I'm immediately welcomed with a full frontal assault. This probably explains why I've never been able to roast a complete marshmallow. As soon as I get my marshmallow perfectly positioned on the end of my stick, I'm assaulted. If there is other smoke in the area, it will rush over and join in the assault. It apparently senses when there is gagging and choking nearby.

Refusing to admit defeat, I circle the campfire. The smoke follows me, continuing its relentless assault. Choking and flailing my arms, I peer through the cloud with reddened, watery eyes, looking for the flame. At the sight of the flame, I joust at it with my stick and marshmallow. I keep jousting at the flame as I continue circling the campfire. By the time my marshmallow is half roasted, I've fled to the car, seeking refuge.

Eating a half roasted marshmallow in your car while you wait for your red, stinging eyes to quit watering will give you a demented, twisted view of camping. But camping is not always like this. It can be far worse.

I prefer something far better. I remembered seeing a picture of a happy camper years before. It was in a camping magazine. The young man was smiling and seemed very happy as he erected his tent with a remote while sitting in the warmth of his car. He went on to tell how this tent would withstand floods, hurricanes, nuclear war and teenagers.

This was my picture of camping. Sure, the picture may have been a bit distorted. But I liked it. His eyes were crystal clear as he dined on a fully roasted marshmallow.

Then I realized the knowledge I could gain from spending time around people who were happy campers. I just had to find them. So, one summer, I began my search. By the end of the summer, I had spotted several Sasquatch, but no happy campers. I did run into a few campers, but they were cold and wet, and trying to light a fire with soggy matches. Just to be sure, I asked, "Any happy campers here?" They made several threatening gestures as they ran me out of camp.

The following summer I continued my quest for the happy camper. A golden opportunity arose when I was mistakenly invited to go camping with our youth group. Arriving at our destination, the air was filled with heightened expectations, along with a plague of swarming mosquitoes.

I knew I could learn a lot about happy camping from our leader, Archie. What could make a person happier, than leading an incorrigible group of pre-teenage boys into the wilderness, unless he was planning on leaving us there? Looking into Archie's eyes, I was certain I could see the peaceful gaze of a happy camper. As we unloaded our gear and started to set up camp, I could sense a significant upcoming event---probably all the knowledge I was about to gain from spending time around our leader. It was just about this time that I took a step backward and sat squarely on Archie's fishing pole, promptly dividing it into two equal parts. As I looked into his eyes, they were missing the peaceful gaze of the happy camper. I stepped forward for a better look. It appeared the gaze had been replaced by a glare. Then I noticed his muscles twitching. I could feel an adrenaline rush coming on as I backpedaled slowly, looking for an open space. When I spotted the open space, I took all of it. As I bolted from camp, I realized that finding a happy camper was not going to be an easy task.

To this day, Archie hasn't invited me fishing again. And I know he has two perfectly good poles. It doesn't matter if they're a little short. The fish don't know the difference.

My search for the elusive happy camper continued after marriage.

For our first vacation, I suggested to my wife that we try camping. I depressed, I mean, impressed her with my backyard and vacant lot credentials. Her primary experience was 5-star, luxury suite hotels; not much to build upon. I tried to convince her there were many happy campers in our midst. I thought, if anything could bond the relationship of newlyweds, it would be camping, especially if we could get involved in a happy camper's group.

Connie was skeptical. She knew happy and five-star hotels went together, but she didn't know about happy and camping. It didn't sound right to her. But after a brief period of weeping and carrying on, lasting no longer than an hour or so, I convinced her that this would be good.

The next day, I looked for a tent with a remote. Not finding it, I took a couple of dollars out of savings and invested in a cozy little pup tent.

"Why didn't you buy a two-man tent?" Connie asked. "We're a bit larger than pups."

"This will be romantic," I said unconvincingly.

Thinking ahead, I also surprised her with bikes for each of us. I had seen many campers riding bikes, with all they needed right on the bike. I thought *if this works out as well as I have planned, eventually we won't need the car. It will just be the two of us, our bikes, and all our gear.* I could feel my adrenaline starting to pump with the heightened expectations as I comforted Connie in her distress.

Before embarking on our vacation of a lifetime, I suggested we try the bikes. Being skeptical of my intent, and cautious about exercise, Connie said, "I hope this isn't going to be the **Tour de France**."

"Not at all," I reassured her, "just a little **Tour de Neighborhood**."

After coasting down and walking up several hills in the area, Connie said, "I think I might do better on a stationary bike, as long as I don't have to use the pedals."

"You will have a hard time keeping up with me on a stationary bike, "I explained.

The day for our departure finally arrived. After diverting my wife's attention with some chocolate, I fastened the bikes to the bike rack on the trunk. Then I went down my checklist, making sure we had everything we needed for our first night in camping heaven. *"Bikes, two sleeping bags, tent*; yep, we've got everything," I assured Connie.

Along the way, we stopped occasionally to ride our bikes.

"When are we going to take the bikes off the rack?" Connie asked.

"When we get out of all this tar and gravel," I answered.

We finally arrived at our destination for the evening. I looked around to see if we might be near any happy campers, but everyone was already asleep.

We squeezed into our cozy little tent and lay down. "I'd better get our sleeping bags," I said, as I jumped up and ran back to the car.

After getting settled, I thought how pleasant to be away from all the distractions of a hotel: TV, air conditioning, running water, comfortable beds with a mint on your pillow....We were well on our way to becoming happy campers, until morning.

The next morning dawned bright and early; well, early, but not bright.

"Why do we have wet sleeping bags?" asked my wife, cleverly hiding her irritation behind a frown. "Did we get running water overnight?"

This gave me the perfect opportunity to help her increase her camping savvy.

"It's *'dew seepage'*", I answered.

"What's *'dew seepage'*?" she asked.

"During the night, dew settles on the tent. It seeps through the material and hangs on the inside, like a bat hanging in a cave. It stays there until you accidentally bump the tent, which then produces a flash flood, sweeping you out of the tent and several miles down a newly-formed creek. Now, we better see if we can find our tent."

Going bump in the night did not move her toward happy camper status. In fact, she looked much like those people who had run me out of camp.

I figured I'd give her a little time to forget this night and, several years down the road, continue my pursuit of the "Happy Camper."

Years later, I discovered a happy camper in my own backyard. It was my cousin, Lester. "I was in town on business," he said. "I didn't want to wake you up when I stopped. Since I carry a sleeping bag for special occasions, I decided I would overnight in your backyard."

"I'm sure it was a special occasion when the sprinkler system went on," I answered.

"It's just one of those amenities of backyard camping."

"Well, you'd better come in and dry off."

During breakfast, we reminisced about our backyard campouts when we were kids.

Then Lester informed me that he had gotten into extreme camping. (And my wife considered any camping extreme.)

I had no idea what was involved in extreme camping. I thought he was camping on the face of a calving glacier, or inside the crater of an erupting volcano, or even on the crumbling banks of a raging river, but I discovered it was far more extreme. Lester had given up five-star hotels for a sleeping bag and a good soccer field.

"There are some who think I'm just being cheap," he said.

"I would probably add 'deluded' in there," I answered. "Of course, I haven't experienced the true comfort of a freshly mowed soccer field."

He admitted it was sometimes difficult getting to sleep with all the cheering. "But it quiets down after the game," he said. "And I know the location of all the sprinklers."

If the weather is poor, Lester resorts to mobile camping. We're not talking forty feet of luxury in a sun-drenched oasis. We're talking fourteen feet of cramped compact in the pouring rain, in a Wal-Mart parking lot. Lester says he's spent so many nights in his car that he's had the locks changed. Now he can use a hotel key card.

He tells me he even has maid service. He uses **Mobile Maids**, a maid service that caters to people who sleep in their cars. Every day they come by to clean and vacuum. Then they make your sleeping bag. He says some even turn down the top of the bag and leave a mint on his pillow.

He's had some problems with the police ignoring his "*Do Not Disturb*" sign hanging on the outside of his car door. He said he does his best to ignore the bright lights shining in the window, but it's the pounding on the car that keeps him awake.

One night, Lester was really embarrassed. He'd forgotten to display his "Do Not Disturb" sign. One of the Mobile Maids was driving by and noticed it said "*Maid May Clean Car.*" While she was trying to get in, the car alarm went off, which attracted the police, and all the lights. He said it took him a long time to get back to sleep. Then he forgot to set his alarm, and overslept. When he woke up, he was riding behind a tow truck. He said the gas was cheap, but the room was a bit pricey.

Lester says that's why it's so much easier camping in a driveway. The sound of a honking horn, as people are trying to leave for work in the morning, is the perfect alarm clock.

When Lester flies and has to rent a car, he's found a company called **Cruise-N-Snooze**. You can not only sleep in the car, but it comes with a sleeping bag.

On a rare occasion, Lester will stay overnight in a hotel. He likes to stay in hotels where pets are welcome. If they refuse to stay, he goes back to the car.

One night, several pets followed him. They wanted to sleep in the car. He said that would be too extreme. He would prefer sharp rocks and pine needles.

"I've given up a few hotel amenities," Lester says, "such as fire alarms going off in the middle of the night or spending the night in an elevator on the 16th floor. But for a happy camper, it's worth it."

Dooley

I had to pick up a few groceries. Because of my shopping allergies, I took the kids along to assist me. They think shopping is fun. They're also looking for possible treats; *gummy bears, chocolate-covered sardines, frozen larvae yogurt*. You know, everything kids like.

We were greeted at the store entrance by two, young children, armed with a box of free kittens. I would have preferred girl scouts armed with cookies. Why hadn't my GPS warned me of this obstruction? Furthermore, there were no "**alerts**" that free kittens were being given away. The kittens completely sidetracked the kids. They forgot about the gummy bears, chocolate-covered sardines, and the frozen larvae yogurt. Why wasn't someone who had lived their life under the iron paw of a cat, standing in the parking lot with a bull horn, warning everyone of this trap?

So there I stood, gazing into the box with my kids and listening to a doctoral thesis on the merits of pet ownership. Soon I heard a still, small voice that proceeded to crescendo into a loud, whining vocal duet. "Daddy, can we have a kitten?" "What about the gummy bears and frozen larvae yogurt?" "No, we want a kitty," they chimed in unison.

For years, I had been told that to be a no-pet family was un-American. "Not having a pet can leave your children emotionally scarred," I was informed by an addicted cat lover. "Do you want your children to carry those scars with them for the rest of their lives?"

"No, just until they leave home," I answered.

I wanted to dangle a chocolate-covered sardine in front of the kids, hoping to detract them from the kittens, but I was overcome with guilt.

It was this burden of guilt, along with a little wailing and gnashing of teeth from my kids, which led me to say, "Yes, you may have a kitten."

After all, to be in a home without shedding hair, shredded sofa ends, and sneezing guests, is to be unloving, uncaring, insensitive, and probably in need of immediate psychiatric care. It obviously shows a wanton disregard for the welfare of your children, not to mention the emotional scars. Not wanting my emotionally scarred children to accuse me of wanton disregard, I decided what better way to teach them about responsibility, than caring for a pet.

We named the cat "Dooley." I was about to fall under the paw.

I knew I met the requirements for owning a pet. I knew nothing.

Wanting Dooley to think I was a leading expert on the cat world, I determined to learn all I could about these fickle fur balls. I wanted to be in control.

The first lesson I learned? I was not in control. I was just a pawn in the cat's kingdom, to be moved at his will. Next time I would go to a store where the kids were giving away free warthogs.

Having known several cat owners in my lifetime, I knew I would have to live with rejection. Most cat owners thrive on it. They aren't happy unless they get a pink slip, lose their job, or have a door slammed in their face. They will only accept no for an answer.

Shortly after arriving home, Dooley set up headquarters in my favorite chair.   Then he went outside to stake his claim to the property. (I was hoping he would include me in his Will.)

Cats stake their claim by *"marking"* their territory. *"Marking"* is done by scratching, rubbing up against something, or spraying. This is a major problem. You have no idea where the cat scratched, rubbed, or sprayed. But he has just defined his territory with an invisible boundary line that runs around your property. Only your cat knows the location of this line. That bothers me. I hate not knowing. I want to know the boundaries. I'm outside, smelling, looking for scratch marks, or any hair lost in rubbing. The cat is sitting there with a smug look. He isn't telling.

Once a cat establishes his boundaries, anything crossing into forbidden territory, including a slug looking for excitement, sets off a high frequency alarm, which only your cat can hear. This informs your cat of an intruder. This raises the hair on your cat's back, and leads to loud screeching which raises the hair on your back and sets off every car alarm in the neighborhood, alerts security, and attracts the police in full riot gear.

If I knew the location of this line, I would dig it up, bury it, burn it, spray it, mow it; whatever is necessary to shut it down. I would replace it with my own sign...**Beware of flying cat. Proceed at your own risk.** But knowing that few cats would pay attention to the sign, I decided that a ten foot high cement barrier surrounding the house would be more effective.

If you let your cat outside, and your home is not surrounded by the *"Great Wall,"* you should be prepared for the occasional territorial disagreement with other nearby cats. These disagreements are usually settled by a lot of hissing, loud screeching, flying claws and biting. **NEVER** try to break up a fight with your hands. If you try this, it means you are exceedingly stupid, and you won't need your hands in the foreseeable future.

Cats are predators. They love to hunt. Dooley was no different. He would display his predatory skills by hiding and waiting for his prey. When it passed by, he would jump out and latch onto it with his claws. I was constantly reminding him that I did not qualify as prey.

Once a cat has their prey, their natural instinct is to pull it to their belly while on their back. They will then kick with their back legs, along with shaking and biting the prey. It's good if you have a small toy, such as a dead mouse, for the cat to use as practice. If the dead mouse has decayed to the point of being useless, the cat is perfectly content to use your arm. If you want to avoid shredded flesh and puncture wounds, you can wrap your arm with several layers of duct tape. Otherwise, you will need a first aid kit and bandages.

Dooley was always trying to impress me with his hunting skills. He would bring home mice, shrews, and the occasional bird, and deposit them on the front porch. If the door was open, he would deposit them in the house. I would have been impressed if he would have brought home an elk. I would have been more impressed if he had deposited it in the freezer; but mice, shrews, and an occasional bird? I could've brought them home.

To keep their claws sharp for hunting, cats love to scratch. Those of you who have filleted sofas and chairs know this.

A scratch is their autograph. They are more than willing to sign your arm and any nearby furniture. If you want to protect your couch and other furniture, cover them with aluminum foil. If this is too much trouble, look for someone who makes aluminum sofas. If you want to protect yourself from scratches, check with someone who does aluminum foil body wraps.

In between shredding furniture and defending his territory, Dooley loved play time, although he didn't do well with games of Fetch. He would watch me chase a stick and bring it back, but he wasn't going to engage himself in such silliness.

He also found "**Spin the Cat**" annoying. My son-in-law, who refuses to be named, had no idea the cat was sleeping in the dryer when he, unknowingly (those are his words), ran him on "*perma* *press."* When he heard the tumbling, he thought it was his wife's tennis shoes. But tennis shoes don't sound like a distressed cat. When Michael realized the cat was doing gymnastics in the dryer, he opened the door. Within a couple hours Dooley had regained his balance. Michael said if he had known the cat was in the dryer, he would have run it on the *"fur"* cycle.

During Dooley's reign of power, I learned that cats love *"Dodge Car."* It's a cat's version of *"Dodge Ball."* They play the game to increase their speed, agility, quickness, and eye/paw coordination. The object of the game is to see how long you can stare into the headlights of an oncoming vehicle before scooting to the other side of the road. To add suspense to the game, you may run into the middle of the road, give a couple good body fakes (one way, then the other), seeing if you can cause the oncoming vehicle to swerve around you. You get two points for crossing the road and a five point bonus for causing the vehicle to swerve. If you try the body fake, and the vehicle doesn't swerve, you lose. Game over. Fortunately, Dooley preferred **Catopoly**, a cat lover's version of **Monopoly**. (Yes, Catopoly is a real board game.)

The longer Dooley ruled, the more I learned about cats. I discovered from watching a documentary that having a cat is good therapy in the war against aging. Petting your cat can add several years to your lifespan. Note: This does not work if you are allergic to cats. If you experience swollen, red, itchy, watery eyes, nasal congestion, chronic sore throat, coughing, sneezing, wheezing, or loss of life, consult your doctor. He may advise you to move, and let the cat have the house. If you experience loss of life, someone else will have to move you.

Not being allergic to cats, I was always looking for Dooley so I could get in a few good strokes. He tried to hide, hoping he would outlive me, and enjoy his remaining years in quiet solitude. But I refused to give up. I'd come home for lunch and spend the entire hour petting him. Then I'd go back to work starving. If I woke up in the middle of the night, I would pet him. The more time I spent petting him, the more exhausted I became. I was aging rapidly. If I kept this up, the cat would still be around long after I was gone. I finally decided I would be happy with a very short life. At least I would outlive the cat, hopefully.

I also learned that your personality often resembles the personality of your pet. My wife had suspected this for some time. "It makes perfect sense," she said. "You're always lying around until you smell food or hear pans rattling around in the kitchen. Then you instantly snap to attention. I just hope you don't start coughing up hairballs."

So petting your cat may increase your lifespan, but if you're going to spend that time coughing up hairballs, you might want to settle for the short life, or live by yourself.

If you truly want to know your cat, you need to understand his body language. This will make you aware of his needs. For example, if his ears are lying flat, hair standing straight up, tail six times its normal size, he's in a crouching position with claws extended, and you can hear a hissing sound, it probably means you forgot to feed him, and may be in imminent danger. At this time, you should begin backing very slowly toward the door, avoiding any quick movements, which could cause him to use your body as a scratching post. When you get outside, quickly shut the door. Then look for an open window and throw in a can of food. He can open it himself. After he has eaten, ask him if you can come back in if you'll promise never to forget again.

Cats take eating very seriously. Dooley was no exception. One evening, my friend, Dave, came by the house with some freshly caught crab. Although Dave is questionable, crabs are always welcome in our home. So I invited them in. Then I invited Dave to join them in the kitchen.

I placed the four crabs in the utility sink. Dooley had been resting, in preparation for his next feeding, when the smell of fresh seafood caught his attention. He jumped up onto the sink for a better look. He was impressed! Here was a four-course seafood delight, inviting him to dinner. He should have declined the invitation. But he had never tried crab, so now was the perfect time for a sample.

Eyeing an easy catch, Dooley jumped into the sink. The sample was brief. It was quickly followed by a loud commotion. Dooley began ricocheting around the sink like a pinball in a pinball machine. One crab had a firm grip on his right hind leg. It looked like rodeo time as Dooley twisted, gnawed, and bucked, trying to shake off the crab. I knew he didn't want this guy on for the full count. So, amidst the screeches and flailing claws, I laid my life on the line to set Dooley free. He cleared the sink by a wide margin and quickly disappeared. Several days later, certain that the crabs were gone, he reappeared. I don't think he ever regained his appetite for seafood.

The episode also strained our relationship. He thought I was using him as crab bait. He had completely forgotten that it was his idea to sample the crab, and that I had rescued him from being a three-legged cat. Still, he gave me the cold shoulder. But being a cat owner, I was used to rejection. I couldn't live without it.

Having Dooley did teach our kids a lot about responsibility. They learned commands like, "Dad, you need to let the cat out", "Dad, you need to let the cat in", "Dad, you need to feed the cat", "Dad, the cat ate something he didn't like. Mom wants you to clean it up", "Dad, can you turn on the TV? Dooley wants to watch '**Animals are Real People**'."

Oh well, what better way to teach your children about responsibility, than caring for a pet.

Who's Not of Camping?

Every year my wife would plan summer vacations for our family. If there's anything that will draw families closer together, it's not family vacations. But they're an excellent stress test. Everyone who passes the test gets to remain in the family for another year.

At the end of each school year, Connie had already planned our summer stress test. Included in the test were the **Backseat Turf Wars**, which the kids trained for during the school year. Also included were the **Tent Wars**, considered epics by our family and all eyewitness accounts. The Tent Wars may have been the greatest spectacle since Cecil B. DeMille's *Ten Commandments*. The tent and I clashed over starring roles. After several scenes, I tried to return the tent and get a refund. But the store's return policy wouldn't accept tents that had anger management problems.

We never ran low on stress. If we did, we would take a stress stop, and add a little more. I would char-broil my uncle's camp lantern or we would listen to our son tell how he was capturing some terrific video with our friend's video camera, when the battery pack got loose, and jumped over the side of a cliff. Then we would watch our daughter compete in the 100-yard dash with a mountain goat, arriving at the car just ahead of the goat. Stress-building should be a part of any good family vacation.

Of course, the highlight of any vacation is capturing it on film. Unfortunately, most of ours refused to be captured.

One summer we were touring Old Fort Edmonton in northern Alberta, Canada. My wife was on point with the camera, getting some of the best pictures she had never taken. That's right! At the end of our tour, she discovered there was no film in the camera. It provided us with some excellent bonus stress. The kids and I threw in a little extra by reminding her that it wasn't a self-loading camera. We also made a few other light-hearted comments, which I won't mention here.

As we left the park, the kids walked behind me. I walked slowly since I could find no one to walk behind. Once our fears of bodily harm subsided, we joined Connie in the car. Driving off, I was certain we had lost a trip planner, but gained a few terse, short sound bites. But there was only silence. After a couple days, Connie was speaking again. We had our trip planner back. The kids and I exhaled.

Returning home from vacation with the entire family was considered an act of God, worthy of a call from the President, inviting us to the White House to honor our achievement.

To commemorate our trip, we hung several empty picture frames on the wall. They drew more attention than the pictures we had captured. All the frames were labeled with historic sites of Old Fort Edmonton. Friends looked long and hard, especially hard, at the empty frames.

"These are from our trip to Edmonton," I explained. "They were taken without film."

"Very creative," one of them said.

"I like what you've done," said another.

They could only imagine what Old Fort Edmonton looked like in the 1800's.

Before the "Tent Wars," our vacations often meant traveling to Nebraska to visit my wife's parents. Along the way, we would stop and visit friends, at least those who would let us stay. After they quit answering our knocks at their door and turned a deaf ear to our whimpering, I decided it was time to take matters into my own hands. We would try camping. I had completely forgotten that my romantic vision of camping was no match for the reality of it. This is probably why my wife was glad it was my idea. She didn't want the blood of camping on her hands.

Being the All-American family that we were, I felt we needed to enjoy a part of our vacation each year in the great outdoors. I could even see our names emblazoned in the *"Who's Who of Camping."*

"But Dad," our kids pleaded, "what about others enjoying the great outdoors; like *mosquitoes*, *snakes*, and **BEARS**!"

Connie may have sided with the kids but, fortunately, her amnesia from child rearing erased all memories of past camping experiences.

Apparently feeling sorry for the kids, and thinking the four of us would have to sleep in a pup tent, my mother bought us a large family tent. "Mom, we will never have a family that large," I said.

"You will appreciate the space," she answered.

It was a heavy canvas tent, made to last. The question was whether I would last, trying to raise it.

Arriving home, we laid out the tent in the backyard. "I don't think we can put this up without a building permit," I said. My mother took one look at the tent and immediately sought refuge in the house. My wife could sense trouble brewing, so she stayed inside and left the tent and me alone, to work out our differences.

There was relative calm until I began to hoist the tent into an upright position. That's when it turned on me. It wasn't long before the neighbors heard a strange noise and looked outside, only to see a large tent thrashing about on the ground. By the time they arrived, the tent was barely moving, collapsed around me like it was guarding its kill. I was still alive, but reduced to a weakened state; suffering from heat exhaustion, and hoarse from begging the canvas monster to spare my life.

With the neighbor's help, I managed to erect the monster. Then I invited them camping. They declined.

My first opportunity to demonstrate my tent-raising skills came in the Colorado Rockies. We arrived at our destination by mid-afternoon so I could have the tent up by nightfall. After pulling it off the car roof, I rolled it out on what could have been mistaken for a rock quarry.

As I started to assemble the tent, a crowd began to gather, apparently hoping for a How-to lesson in raising a canvas tent the size of a small apartment. In a matter of minutes, their demeanor went from curious to rolling-on-the-ground, belly laughs.

"This is embarrassing," said my wife. "Why couldn't we have found some place where there were no people?"

"Who would hear our screams if this thing went down?" I answered. "We could be trapped under this canvas for days with no way out."

Stepping around those who continued to roll on the ground, I finally completed the tent-raising, sometime after dark. Proud that I had completed my project, I wanted to hand out memorial tent pegs, but everyone was sound asleep.

As we prepared for bed, my wife asked, "Where is Justin's bedding?"

I checked the car, and, sure enough, it was home.

"He's a year old; he can sleep with us," I said.

So off to sleep we went, until the middle of the night. The thunder woke us up. Soon, torrential rains were pounding the roof as lightning danced across the sky. Fierce winds buffeted the tent. I was thankful I had taken time to raise a tent that would withstand a storm. It was just about then that everything started to shift. I had prepared it for the wrong storm.

As the tent was shifting, Justin was leaving the sleeping bag. Whisking him back in, we felt the tent collapsing upon us.

Knowing it would be futile to try and raise the tent again in the thunderstorm, we remained where we were until daybreak, when rescuers came and pulled us from the collapsed canvas.

"Being close to people didn't matter," Connie said. "They still didn't hear our screams."

"They were worn out from laughter," I answered.

"Well, I'm worn out from camping," she responded, rather convincingly.

So we took a break from camping for a brief time, probably three to four years. By that time, the memories of our past experience were dimming, so we attempted another round of "**Camping World.**"

For our next foray into outdoor living, we decided to stay inside.

Camping in a tent had humbled us. "Maybe we'll fare better if we camp in our van," I said.

"I agree," said our daughter. "Hopefully, it won't collapse on us."

So we loaded up the van and headed for the mountains, once again, trying to get our names written in the *Who's Who of Camping*.

Since we were in our van and not headlining the entertainment for the evening, we were able to arrive at our campground in the late afternoon. Our later arrival meant we got the last campsite. We all agreed this was far better than having to camp in someone's driveway.

"Look!" yelled the kids. "We're right on the lake!"

Closer inspection revealed a small pond of stagnant water that smelled like a large cesspool.

Not too far away, we noticed some empty buildings. "Must have been the Waste Treatment Plant that's quit giving treatments," said Connie.

"Prime mosquito breeding grounds," I opined.

"That's good," Connie said. "They'll probably be too busy to get over here."

They obviously overheard her and rushed over immediately. Then they signaled to their friends..."*Hey, over here...campsite 65...four people...two children and two adults...adults can feed family of two thousand...children, maybe a thousand.*"

While our culinary institute was dining on marshmallows on a stick, the mosquitoes were feasting on us. They apparently thought it was a buffet because they kept coming back for seconds and thirds.

Having your blood supply reduced to critically low levels by mosquitoes who think they're partaking of the **Fountain of Youth** is distressing enough, but watching them carry on in such a disorderly and unseemly manner was revolting.

We let them sample about twelve different repellents. They loved all of them. Just before they had sucked the remaining life out of us, we stumbled into the van and passed out.

The next morning, we decided it would be best if we chose an activity away from the water and mosquitoes.

"Let's go for a hike," I said.

"Don't we need to carry bear bells?" asked my wife.

"Yes!" I answered emphatically.

Once all of us had our bells, we began hiking along a nearby trail.

After walking a short distance, I heard our daughter. "Why do we need these bells?" she asked. "Is it to scare the bears or to let them know lunch is ready?"

"It's to let them know that we're in the area," I answered.

"Why do they need to know?" questioned Mindy. "Are they expecting us? They should let us know when they're in the area."

"Just stay on the trail, and we'll be fine," I said.

"Do I just keep following these paw prints?" she asked.

"We've probably followed them far enough," I answered. "Let's head back to camp."

We spent the afternoon reading in the van and watching the mosquitoes drool on the windows while they waited for dinner. We weren't doing take-out.

By early evening, the mosquitoes had given us up for dead. So they left in search of new blood. Having been in lockdown most of the afternoon, we were all getting hungry. I suggested building a nice campfire and frying some fish, but we had no fish, and my wife didn't trust my campfires. We looked for the marshmallows, but they had disappeared in the *Great Mosquito Invasion.* "Okay, it looks as though we'll have to forage for some edible plants and insects," I said.

"We'll need something to go with our insect dish," said my wife, her voice dripping with enough sarcasm that it was running down the front of her sweatshirt. "I think we should go into town and forage for some pizza," she insisted.

"That's not roughing it in the wild outdoors," I answered.

"Well, I'm not going to sit out here in the wild outdoors, eating my insects and chewing on a piece of bark," she announced to everyone within hearing distance.

"Okay, okay," I said, peeking out from behind a tree.

It wasn't long before we were all foraging on pizza at a local eatery. The edible insect topping was especially tasty. After returning to our campsite, I thought I would light our lantern and relax with a good book.

I had borrowed the lantern from my uncle. He had carefully explained how to light it. I should have listened carefully. I remembered him saying, "It's really very simple; a six year old could do it." So I skipped the "careful explanation" I had forgotten, and struck a match to light the wick. It wouldn't light. "Maybe you should try lighting it over the fire pit and not on the picnic table," my wife suggested. (She always seemed to sense when trouble was brewing.)

"It's easier on the picnic table," I answered.

I tried another match; nothing; another; nothing. I looked for a six year old, but there were none around. I pushed, twisted, and prodded anything that could be pushed, twisted, and prodded.

With the futile strike of every match, I started talking to the lantern. The lantern remained silent. I struck another match... nothing. I turned up the volume. My son thought this was possibly better than my Christmas tree talk routine. Then I looked up and saw other campers, along with several marmots, starting to move in for a look. I could sense I was, once again, becoming the entertainment. Connie and the kids had taken shelter in the van. They were peering out the windows, hoping the people wouldn't think we were related.

After a book of matches, I finally succeeded in lighting the lantern. It was lighting overkill. The entire lantern was engulfed in flames. I shouldn't have been surprised. Most of my fires exhibit a complete lack of control---possibly the reason my wife doesn't trust them. I feared the fire would burn the picnic table to the ground, then jump a nearby creek and torch several thousand acres. Not wanting to be the feature story on the national news, I sprang into action. I sprang onto the table and *"danced with flames."*

With quick action, I managed to stomp out the fire before it burned the table to the ground and spread through the campground, looking for the nearby creek. Once again, I had given everyone an entertaining evening with my camp routines.

As the ovation died down, I gave a few guttural sounds and resigned myself to a night without reading by the lantern.

We eventually worked our way home, and waited for a call from the President, inviting us to the White House.

We had now done tent camping and van camping. Surely, we were getting closer to being enshrined in the *Camper's Hall of Fame*.

After several more years had elapsed for sufficient memory loss, I suggested our next family adventure. "On our next ten day vacation, let's divide our time between camping and hotels."

"Divide it right down the middle," Connie answered, "Nine nights, hotel; one night, camping; unless that's too much camping."

We let the kids choose our destination since we thought it might be our last family trip together; although we thought that after every vacation.

They chose the Canadian Rockies.

As we made our way toward the mountains, no one mentioned the "B" word, but we were heading into prime bear territory.

The second day out we noticed an ominous-looking sign along the highway; "**BEAR WARNING—DANGEROUS**--if you see a bear, remain in your car at all times." Next to the sign, they had a picture of a bear for those who might have trouble identifying one. Fortunately, I already had a picture of a bear in my billfold.

Not long after passing the sign, we noticed a long line of cars pulled off on the side of the road, a sure sign of bears nearby. As my wife was reminding us about the "bear warning" sign, I pulled off the road, behind the last car. Then the kids and I did what everyone else had done; we grabbed our cameras, threw open the doors, and sprinted, to get in position for the best bear picture of the year; one we could send to **National Geographic**.

At the same time, we heard Connie yelling, "Get back here and shut all the doors, in case the bear circles back!"

After getting some terrific pictures of the backs of other people taking pictures, we continued down the road.

That evening we camped in the mountains. We arrived after dark, when all the other campers were asleep as I was just too tired to entertain. While I tried to quell my own family's laughter, I worked to erect the tent. By now, I was able to do it in an hour.

While putting up the tent, I noticed there were locks on all the garbage cans. Our daughter became concerned. "I know **PEOPLE** aren't getting into the garbage," she said.

I was also concerned, because I'm extremely sensitive to marauding bears, especially those marauding at my campsite; a little hokey-pokey, maybe; but marauding, no.

As soon as we bedded down, I began wishing for my own garbage can with a locked lid over my head. Lying nestled in my sleeping bag, I felt like a Philly cheesesteak. I was just hoping bears didn't like cheesesteaks.

"Aren't we supposed to hang food in a tree, away from bears?" Connie asked.

"There wasn't enough rope for all of us," I answered. "Besides, I can't sleep hanging in a tree."

I remembered the admonition to remain in my car if I saw a bear. "What if I see a bear while I'm curled up in my sleeping bag?" I wondered. "Would he let me go sit in the car to watch the hokey-pokey?" I knew if there was any marauding, I wanted to watch it in my rear view mirror.

The next day I was exhausted. I had to drive with one eye because the other eye had stayed open all night, watching for bears. I was thankful none of the animals I had seen that night matched the picture in my billfold.

About mid-day, we stopped at a nice hotel. I had to rest the eye I had been using to drive. As I was falling into a deep slumber, I finally realized we would never make it into the *"Who's Who of Camping,* but I was certain we qualified for the *"Who's Not of Camping."*

This Old Farmhouse

Parking the car, I got out and scanned our new home. The old Cape Cod style farmhouse was a local landmark. It was considered a collector by those who collect old farmhouses.

Once a bustling dairy farm, it now sat empty, surrounded by tall grass and wild blackberry bushes winding their way through the trees in an old orchard, next to the house.

Some said the house was haunted, but it was really just a farmhouse that needed a little TLC. Okay, a lot of TLC. Like most men, I loved the idea of trying my skills as Mr. Fix It. Like most women, my wife loved things already fixed. In between was tension.

"This old farmhouse will give me the perfect opportunity to work with my hands," I told her.

"If you want to work with your hands, you should consider sign language," she said. "I'm certain there would be less tension."

While Connie and the kids sat nervously in the car, I continued eyeing the old farmhouse, thinking of the opportunities it would provide for family bonding.

I also thought of the fond memories I had of life on Gramps' ranch.

"I want you kids to enjoy the same rich experiences of life on the farm that I had growing up," I told them.

"Are those the same rich experiences that almost maimed you for life?" my wife asked.

"Look, the scars are hardly noticeable. Sure, I may have an occasional panic attack when I dream of the barn burning and the evil rooster chasing me, and almost drowning in Gramps' lake, but..."

Our daughter interrupted. "Dad, I think Justin and I would rather endure the experiences of our friends."

"Don't you want to experience pioneer life in a 1930's farmhouse?"

"We can read about that in our textbooks. I don't think we need a hands-on experience."

"Great! Then we all agree! This is going to be our new home."

I've continued to leave the lines of communication open, in case the kids want to talk someday.

The day arrived for our move into the old farmhouse. It had no insulation, no electric heat, and single-pane windows that could have been upgraded to chicken wire. We would enjoy the great outdoors, indoors. It had an old wood stove that was large enough to hold a small forest. This would allow us to cut and stack wood together; the perfect recipe for family bonding.

I was looking forward to the challenges of the old farmhouse. I didn't have to wait long. The first challenge met us on our arrival. The front door wouldn't let us in. "With your experience in woodshop, maybe you could *SAND* it down," said my wife. I loved her sense of humor. After jiggling a key in the lock for approximately 20 minutes and politely threatening the door with a hole in its midsection, it let us in. The next challenge was close behind. As I shut the door, the doorknob on both sides fell off. Fortunately I had a screwdriver, which I always carried with me for my encounters with missing doorknobs. With the screwdriver, I was able to twist the lock assembly and open the door.

More challenges followed. We quickly learned the farmhouse had not been wired for modern conveniences. We didn't know *lights* were considered a modern convenience. The slightest provocation would cause everything to go dark..."You kids need to turn off the television. I'm going to run the dishwasher," my wife would say.

Other times we would make choices..."Should we do the wash and read by candle light, or should we turn on the lights and wear the same clothes tomorrow?"

It soon became evident that unexpected challenges would be lurking throughout the old farmhouse.

One morning we were awakened by a scream from our daughter. "There's a bird on my bedpost!" she yelled.

I jumped out of bed and ran upstairs. Perched on her bedpost was the **Townsend Warbler**; a rare find, indeed.

"Wow!" I exclaimed. "These birds are usually found outdoors."

I was hoping the Audubon Society wouldn't find out. I feared they might try to get her room designated as a bird sanctuary. Then we'd have to worry about "birders" hiding in her closet, waiting for another sighting of the **Warbler**.

I would have to coax the bird out of the house before there was a knock at our door from an Audubon representative. I knew that extreme calm was necessary in negotiating an exit. Never send your cat to do the negotiating. This can result in a large cleaning bill. You must talk the bird out slowly and deliberately. Be sure to have all the doors and windows open. You can always wrap up in a blanket if it is sub-freezing, and you have to wait several days for the bird to make his travel plans. Thankfully, we didn't endure a long wait. Our **Townsend Warbler** flew out an open window. I love a smart, quick-thinking bird.

We must have been on a migratory flight path, because we had birds visit on several occasions. I was waiting for a migration of Canadian Geese to stop for lodging on their way back to Canada. If I would have known we were going to be a wildlife refuge, I would have offered the birds a key to the house.

Each new day brought more adventure. One night, as I was falling asleep in my recliner, Connie said to me, "I think a bird just flew from the kitchen into the dining room."

"It's probably heading north for the winter," I mumbled.

"Well, it's not going to get far in the dining room."

I got up to help the bird with directions. There was no bird. So I went into the kitchen. There was still no bird.

Then I checked the utility, next to the kitchen. No bird. Just as I turned to go back into the living room, I spotted a bat hanging on one of the cupboards. I would have rather seen a two-toed sloth hanging there. This is because I don't like bats. I'm convinced it's a vampire bat; a hanging blood bank. "We don't have vampire bats around here," laughed my wife.

"Well, this one didn't tell me where he lived, and I'm not taking chances."

So I wrapped a towel around my neck. Then I thought: our cat! What if he goes after the bat? I knew the mice were safe in the house, but I didn't know about the bat. Then another thought hit me; what if the bat goes after the cat? Maybe I should wrap a towel around the cat's neck. I pictured the cat and bat chasing each other throughout the house....utility, kitchen, dining room, living room, bedrooms...

I knew this: I wasn't going to bed until the bat was gone. So I came up with a bat evacuation plan.

"Get the cat out of the house," I yelled to my wife.

"Why?" she asked.

"I don't want the cat chasing the bat around the house."

"The cat is not going to chase the bat," answered my wife, laughing hysterically.

"Okay, what about the bat chasing the cat around the house?"

She couldn't answer. She was laughing too hard.

Since she was disabled with laughter, I would have to take care of this myself.

I would have to confine the bat to the kitchen and utility. I would also have to offer it a way out. So I closed all the doors. But I still had a problem. There was no door between the kitchen and dining room. But there was a doorway, where there had been a door at one time. If I closed that space, the bat couldn't fly into the living and dining area. Then I could go outside and open the back door, off the utility.

But how would I close that space? I know! The bathroom door! I would borrow the bathroom door. I would just have to remember to put it back when I was done.

I quickly ran in and removed the door. It would be a perfect fit for sealing off the dining room. So I ran through the living room with the door, heading for the opening to the kitchen. My wife had not taken the cat outside, so the cat was roaming free, looking puzzled as to why I was running through the living room with the bathroom door and a towel wrapped around my neck. The cat thought he would wander into the kitchen for a bite to eat, but I beat him to the opening and slammed the door in place, making sure there were no cracks for him to get through.

"Can you come and hold this door in place while I run around to the back of the house and open the back door?" I asked my wife. She pulled herself off the floor, where she has been rolling in laughter. While she held the bathroom door, I ran around and opened the back door. A short while later the bat disappeared. I was through with the cat and the bat. And I was exhausted. It was time for bed.

My wife was still laughing as I fell asleep.

The old farmhouse convinced me we could have a primetime reality show, although it probably wouldn't have been suitable for children.

After the winter cold, power outages, birds in the house, and a bat in the utility, along with other assorted surprises, I waited for my next challenge. The wait was short-lived. It began with a gurgling toilet. I was hoping it wouldn't require immediate attention. The toilet was already on shaky flooring. But until I could do a complete bathroom renovation, I was getting a quarter a ride for it.

Just as I was about to raise the price to thirty-five cents, it demanded immediate attention. I was having a drain problem. I don't like drain problems. I decided to check the septic tank. After some digging, I found the cement cover to the tank. In the process of removing the cover, it got loose and went down like the Titanic. Uh, Oh! As I stood, looking into the tank, I could see the problem. It was full. Nothing was moving. Not good! I sacrificed a toilet bowl, hoping to appease the god of the drain field. He just scoffed in mock laughter.

I finally sent out a *PDS*...**Plumber's Distress Signal.** This meant waving a plunger while dancing around the septic tank in hip waders. While I was waiting for someone to answer my distress call, I realized I needed to replace the tank cover. I didn't want someone to take a misstep and find themselves backed up.

So I made a new cement cover. In the process, I overlooked a couple, minor details. First, I should have done my work closer to the tank hole. Secondly, I should have used better judgment regarding the thickness of the concrete. The cover became a landmark memorial in the backyard, dedicated to those who had fought in the "septic tank" wars. I settled for a piece of plywood over the hole.

I was finally rescued by a good friend, Miles. With his help, we restored the drain field. A sense of normalcy returned to the old farmhouse...or whatever normalcy one could get out of an old farmhouse.

After re-doing the drain field, any time I saw someone wearing a shirt that said "**No Fear,**" I thought, "That person has never heard a gurgling toilet." You never forget that terrifying sound!

Not long after the **Great Spring Backup**, I decided it was time to remodel the bathroom. I had watched enough home improvement programs on television to mistakenly think I could complete my project in less than an hour, without the commercials.

I should have known never to take on a project of this magnitude when my wife was perfectly capable of doing it herself. Nevertheless, I pushed ahead, completely ignoring her pleas for me to seek help. "I know a good counselor," she said, "who's dealt with many husbands who have attempted to renovate a bathroom."

"This is just something I have to do," I answered.

"Alright," she went on, "but don't forget the time you tried removing a hangnail with a table saw."

"That program on bathroom renovations has shown me everything I need to know about a remodel," I said.

"Didn't they also say, 'Don't try this at home?'" Connie continued.

Ignoring logic, common sense and history, I refused to give up on my project. I knew if I quit it would be a blow to my self-image as Mr. Fix-it.

Although there is no reason for remodeling a bathroom, other than strengthening the ties that bind (specifically, a rope around the neck), it did give me time to myself because the rest of the family had taken refuge in a friend's home, citing the wisdom of my former woodshop teacher, **Mr. Greathouse**, who told every student to clear out if I picked up anything other than sandpaper.

During my remodel, I learned there is something a man should never do: **NEVER** tell your wife when you're starting a project. She will instantly set a due date in her mind, and if it's not done by the due date, a change of address may be necessary, with no forwarding address. Certainly you should never suggest another project, unless you have backup protection. You see, most wives forget to take into account your time with the boys, football, hunting, fishing, and just plain laziness. You'd think they'd be more understanding than that.

When I decided to remodel our bathroom, I made the mistake of telling Connie. Of course, seeing the toilet in the living room caught her attention and caused some tension. After she returned from a couple days and nights of binge shopping, I could see something flashing in the bathroom. It was a small neon sign she had hung on the wall. It was flashing the due date.

"Very clever," I told her.

"Just a subtle hint," she answered.

Every day that she insisted I get the bathroom completed, I kept telling her I was right on schedule. She had just failed to recognize one of the laws of nature; you have his and her due dates, and never the two shall meet. "Well, if they don't meet, there's going to be big trouble," she said. I sensed from her comment that there could be big trouble. She also mentioned she was tired of using the restroom at McDonald's, and McDonald's had refused my request to put in a shower. So, as a precautionary safety measure, I changed my due date to match hers. I also wanted to do my share to promote peace on earth. I finished my remodel just as the due date was expiring. I had new life!

After enough time had passed to dull her memory of the bathroom, I approached Connie with my next project. "Is there anything we need to talk about?" I asked.

"Why?" she asked, beginning to tremble.

"I was planning to remodel Mindy's room, and I knew that once I started, we wouldn't be talking for a while." She left immediately for the pharmacy, looking for an anti-remodeling vaccine while our son was calling the locksmith to get a deadbolt lock put on his door.

I used to think remodeling would be fun and easy because I always watched programs on television like *This Old House*, where Bob Vila was always smiling, and the nails went in straight; and everything was done in thirty minutes. Then I discovered remodeling off TV... the darker side of remodeling: grinding your teeth to the gums, talking to your hammer in a high-pitched voice, blowing cold air on hot swollen thumbs, and trying to explain to the hardware man why you're returning a sack full of bent nails..."they weren't strong enough to go in straight." On top of this, your project is taunting you, daring you to come back and finish what you started.

Forget the due date. Let's go test the fishing. I'll just call Bob Vila and have him stop by **THIS** old farmhouse, and finish my project with a smile; and it will be done before I cast my line.

Deep Freeze

I braced myself against the bone-chilling cold. It penetrated every part of my body. I wiggled my toes and fingers to be sure they were still attached. I should have dressed more warmly, but here I was, kneeling in front of the old woodstove in my underwear, trying to start a fire. I struck a match, then another match, but they refused to be lit. I threatened the rest of them with a good hosing if they didn't cooperate. I didn't want to be found in the spring, lying curled up by the old stove, still clutching a box of matches. I finally got one to cooperate. I shared its flame with the newspaper resting amongst the kindling. Then I ran back and jumped in bed, waiting for the fire to start crackling before I added some more wood.

About fifteen minutes later, my wife got up to check the fire. "You'd better come in here and threaten this newspaper," she yelled, shivering in the cold. "The paper didn't stay lit. It looks like it just received some minor smoke damage." I finally resorted to the blow torch, and had a roaring fire within minutes, barely keeping it within the confines of the woodstove.

We had moved into the old 1930's farmhouse in August. By mid-November, we were being assaulted by heavy snow and falling temperatures. Soon we would be in the midst of a record-setting deep freeze. I was hoping to use the challenges of the old farmhouse for family bonding, but I now feared we might crack and shatter before we had a chance to bond.

With no insulation, the cold marched right in and made itself at home. It didn't even have the courtesy to knock first. The cold became so comfortable, I was afraid it would never leave. Our family wondered how long we could survive in cold storage. The kids complained of freezer burn.

With the old woodstove as our only source of heat, we had prepared for the worst. It was far worse. After several licks at the ice on his water bowl, our cat disappeared. We feared his demise. But a week after his disappearance, we received a post card with a paw print from Palm Springs. Cats are so innovative and self-sufficient. We saved the litter box, knowing he would return in the spring.

To combat the deep freeze, I sought the advice of a friend, Flynn Willie, who had experience in cold weather survival training. "You'll never survive the deep freeze in this old farmhouse without 'mind over matter,'" he said bluntly. "Remember how your baseball coach would tell you a broken leg was all in your mind, even if it were pointing in three different directions?" he asked.

"How could I forget?" I answered, resting on a crutch.

"Well, cold is the same. It's a state of mind."

"What about toes that fall off?" I asked. "Is that a state of mind?"

"Absolutely," he answered.

In case he was wrong, I got a box to keep my toes in until they could be re-attached during the spring thaw. It was beginning to look like a long winter.

As the deep freeze intensified, we confronted it with "mind over matter." We discovered that doesn't work when matter is frozen.

Every morning we did penance by walking across frozen floors. "Just once, I would love hot coals," said my wife.

I was glad our family had a large woodstove we could huddle around to stay warm. I was sad when it developed a crack and had to be replaced by a new-fangled E.P.A.-approved woodstove. I was distraught that we had to wait two weeks for our new woodstove. It was our only source of heat. Our rugged individualism would be sorely tested. One morning we had a big frost...the first I'd ever seen in the living room. If we went much longer without heat, I would have to set the furniture on fire. I tried to look on the positive side; we didn't have to keep anything in the freezer.

Our new *"pollution solution"* woodstove finally arrived. It eliminated all the smoke coming out our chimney. Instead, it was re-routed out the back of the stove. "**Wow**," I thought, "I could have saved money by burning the furniture." Fearing I would be transformed into a charcoal figurine, I covered my nose and mouth with a handkerchief while I managed to shut down the fire in the stove.

After a few adjustments, I started another fire. The smoke stayed in the stove. But I wondered where it was going now. Then I went outside. Oh! There it is, coming out our chimney. I breathed a sigh of relief.

Our new woodstove would have fit nicely inside our old woodstove. Now we would have to take turns huddling by the fire. There was barely enough room for the cat. Fortunately, he had left for the winter. The rest of us fought for thawing space.

One morning, after scraping enough frost off the inside of the windows to make a small snowman, Connie said, "I'm tired of the cold." I could sense from her comment that she was tired of the cold.

"Why can't we have a new home?" she pleaded.

"Where would we put the snowman?" I asked. "Anyway, what would I write about; that we're relaxing in our lovely new home, kicking back in a lounge chair, reading a book by the fire?"

"I could write it" she answered.

I tried to explain to her, "People don't want to hear how comfortable you are; they want to hear about your miserable, wretched life, as you struggle against the elements. They want to hear about rugged individualism; surviving a winter in an old farmhouse with barely enough heat to melt the frost on the sofa. So stomp out that fire you started on the carpet, and hand me my gloves so I can start writing. On second thought, I guess I need to go to the library to write."

"Why can't you write here?" she insisted.

"Ink freezes at this temperature," I answered.

When I returned home, Connie was busy filling out papers. "What are those?" I asked.

"Adoption papers," she answered.

"I don't think we can afford more children," I informed her.

"I'm not trying to adopt," she went on. "I'm putting US up for adoption. Hopefully there is someone out there who will take in a family of four, with one request; that we be placed with a family that has heat in every room. And it would be nice if I didn't have to brush my teeth with de-icer."

"Look at the positive side," I said. "The cold has killed all the bugs; the cat has gone south; the mice have frozen to death in the pantry, and the vultures have been grounded because of ice buildup on their wings. Besides, cold is a great preservative. It prevents aging."

"That's because nothing is moving. I'd rather see some moving parts, preferably on a warm, sandy beach in Hawaii."

As the deep freeze continued, we had friends visit. They were apparently hoping for the same rich experiences our kids had enjoyed before they left to live with friends. A cold north wind was blowing when Butch and Ginger arrived.

"Welcome to the old farmhouse," said Connie. "Come on in and get warm." Butch and Ginger stepped inside.

"**Whoa!**" exclaimed Butch, "I may have to go back outside to warm up! I can see why the drapes are hanging at half-mast. Now, where do we get warm?"

"We spend most of our time around this old woodstove," answered Connie. Butch and Ginger raced over to the stove.

"After reading about the farmhouse in Wake's Christmas letter, I thought he was exaggerating about the cold," said Butch. "But now I think he was lying; it's much colder."

"Is it always this cold inside?" Ginger asked.

"Only when it's this cold outside," Connie answered.

After a little more chatter, we all sat down to eat. Dinner was filled with reminiscing and laughter. While eating, Ginger noticed one of our windows. "Oh, Connie, I love what you've done to your windows," she said. "Those ornate etchings are simply beautiful. How did you do it?"

"I didn't," answered Connie. "It's frost."

"Inside?" quizzed Ginger.

"Why do you think Connie told us to finish eating before the food freezes," said Butch in amusement.

After dinner, we spent more time visiting around the woodstove. "I can see why this woodstove is such a great gathering place," said Butch. "I can feel the ice flow in my veins starting to break up."

As we warmed, we continued talking into the late evening until it was time for bed.

"Go ahead and take our room," Connie told Ginger. "It has a warm waterbed." There was no argument.

"I was prepared to offer anything, even our children, just for a warm blanket," said Butch.

Everyone laughed as we reluctantly left our spot near the woodstove.

It wasn't long before we heard the voice of Butch. "I know this sounds silly," he said, "but why is a deer hanging in the utility?"

"He didn't like the waterbed. *Just kidding*! My good friend, Fred, got him while hunting last week. He said the temperature inside the house was the ideal temperature for hanging a deer. So I told him he could hang it here. It would save him money and give me something to write about."

"I like all the lights and colorful ornaments," said Butch. "I could bag a deer that's dressed like a Christmas tree."

107

"Connie did that. She thought he would look better dressed out in Christmas décor. We did have the deer in the living room, but we kept running into him. So we moved him to the utility. Besides, he didn't go with the furniture."

"I don't mind the deer," said Butch. "But if I see his breath, I'm going hunting."

After a final laugh, we turned out the lights and went to sleep.

During the night, the power went out.

The next morning we found Butch and Ginger wrapped up in blankets in the living room. Butch was reading a semi-blackened newspaper. "Yeah, I tried to start a fire," he said. "But I didn't have much success."

"I'm glad I found you before spring," I answered.

"I'm just glad I can see my breath in here," Butch continued. "It's the only way I know I'm alive."

"How did you enjoy the waterbed?" Connie asked.

"Great," said Butch, "Until the power went out. Then it was like sleeping on a floating ice pack. During the night, I dreamed a polar bear was standing at the foot of the bed, waiting for me to stick my head out of the covers, thinking I was a seal. That's probably why I couldn't find the mint you laid on my pillow. I think I offered it to the bear."

It wasn't long before I had a roaring fire in the woodstove. We all took our positions and continued reminiscing about warmer times past.

Since we lived in an area near great crabbing, Butch was insistent about getting a crab or two during their visit. I picked a night when the weather was perfect---a foot of snow on the ground and temperatures hovering near ten degrees. I got out everything we would need, handed Butch his hip waders, and we drove down to the water. After wading out a distance, Butch said, "My legs and feet are starting to get cold and wet."

"Must be that leak I meant to fix," I said. "Just think 'warm.'"

"I'm trying to think 'warm'", said Butch, "but my legs and feet keep arguing with me. They're saying, 'We don't care what you're thinking. We're going numb.'" Not willing to give in to the numbing cold, Butch wandered off in another direction in search of the elusive crab. Soon I heard some commotion and turned around to see Butch skipping across the icy water toward shore, waving a crab in the air for me to see. Excited that Butch had gotten a crab, I began working my way toward shore. When I arrived, Butch was still prancing around showing off his crab. "Nice crab," I said. "Now, if you'll just stop prancing for a moment, we'll get that crab off your finger." After removing the crab and satisfying Butch with multiple re-counts of all his fingers, we drove back to the house. Along the way I said, "Next time, remind me to tell you about the *Fine Art of Crab Handling*.'" Butch didn't hear a word. He was too busy blowing on his swollen finger.

After several days, Butch and Ginger had to leave but said they would take their experiences on the farm with them forever, or until they could find a place to dump them alongside the road.

I felt bad they had to leave so soon. The very next day we had water spraying in the utility and under the house. This signaled the beginning of our annual **Pipe Burst Festival**. The Ice Sculpting competition was always popular. *The Plumber in Ice* was everyone's favorite. Another crowd-pleaser was the *Plumber's Speed Crawl*. In this event, at least six plumbers would position themselves under the local homes. At the sound of rushing water, they would stampede for the exit. (Stampeding on your back can be extremely challenging.) The plumber with the best time reaching the exit received an all-expenses paid trip to the **Plumber's Pipe Wrench Convention** in Drain, Oregon---a real town!

I called our friends to invite them to next year's festival, but the operator kept telling me they had an unlisted number. I finally sent a letter, but it came back, saying they had moved and left no forwarding address. *Maybe they don't want to return*, I thought. No, I'm sure that's just a figment of my imagination, I convinced myself as I inched closer to the woodstove to get warm.

The Perfect Tree

It was three weeks before Christmas. Our family was on our annual hunt for the *"Great Tree,"* when I ran into my good friend, Ozzie. "Still trying to find that perfect tree?" he asked, with a mixture of cynicism and amusement.

"I'm always trying to find that *"elusive"* tree," I answered.

"I once believed it was possible to find one," Ozzie continued, "but my encounter with that branch this past summer, shattered my belief in perfect trees."

It had been a *"summer to remember"* for Ozzie. He and his wife were enjoying an outdoor concert when a slight breeze turned into a stiff wind. The trees surrounding the concert began swaying back and forth. Without warning, a rogue tree hurled one of its branches at Ozzie's wife. Ozzie managed to intercept the branch. For his act of heroism, Ozzie won a two week, all expenses paid, roundtrip ticket to a local hospital. He was thankful the ticket was roundtrip.

He now viewed all trees with suspicion. "You can never trust a tree," said Ozzie. "A tree may stand there smiling at you, but beneath those branches may be a tree with a serious behavior disorder."

Having been slapped around by a number of trees myself, I could understand Ozzie's thinking. Christmas trees can be especially belligerent. You may think you have found the **ONE**, but start spinning it around for a better look and you've got trouble. *"Hey! Stop it! That makes me dizzy! Do it again and you'll get a face full of needles!"*

The challenge of finding the perfect tree has earned me a *"green belt"* in the age-old sport of tree wrestling.

Around the first week of December our family bundles up and goes out in search of that perfect Christmas tree. After a lengthy hunt, we finally get committee approval for a tree.

I want to decorate the tree at the lot, and come by to visit it. It would be much easier than wrestling with the tree at home. Besides, it has a distinct size advantage. The committee overrules me.

So we now have to decide who is going to walk home in the cold, while the tree rides in the car. There isn't enough room for everyone. My son suggests we put the tree on the roof of the car. I tell my son that would scare the sap out of the tree and, besides, I'm not a tree-on-the-roof kind of guy. It has to go in the car.

Our son agrees to wait by the fire in the shed at the tree lot while the tree rides home with the rest of the family. He reminds me to pick him up before the tree wrestling scene. So we open the hatch, put down the back seats, and shove the tree in the car. I drive home with the base of the tree in my right ear. I hope it doesn't leak pitch.

We finally get the tree home. Then I go back to the lot and pick up our son. Once home, I try to stall, hoping Christmas will pass before I have to attempt putting up the tree. But the committee is not going for the stall tactic. So we move all the furniture into the garage to make room for the tree.

Somehow I get the tree into the house. Now I have to saw the base off so it's flat at the bottom, and will stick into the teeth of the tree stand. My wife complains because I'm running the chain saw in the house. I tell her I'm cutting up some table legs for the woodstove.

Just kidding! Now it's time to fit the tree into the tree stand. **Note**: Don't try this at home, alone. This is exactly what the tree wants; you and it alone, where it can turn you into a carpet square.

The tree does not want to go in the tree stand. Even with my *green belt* in Tree Wrestling, the tree is putting up a good fight. I've been slapped several times by good-sized branches. I may have to enlist the aid of a wrestling troupe.

After threats against the life of the tree, it still refuses to go in the tree stand. Oops! The trunk is too big for the stand. I utter several more threats against the tree and the stand. Then I run to the *Tree Stands R Us* store and get the right size.

Another attempt is made to place the trunk into the tree stand. It will fit if I cut off the lower limbs. The committee is getting restless. My wife is concerned that the tree will turn brown and the needles will fall off before I get it into the tree stand. It's going to need water soon.

Now let me regress for a moment. Years ago, this was a simple process. Trees would be stood upright in a bucket. Then the bucket would be filled with rocks, holding the tree upright. If the tree refused to stand up straight, the rocks would be used to stone the tree.

Okay, back to reality. I'm having trouble getting the tree in the correct upright position. The committee goes outside to look for *rocks*, but I don't think they're going to stone the tree. My wife informs me that summer is just around the corner, and the tree is long overdue for water. I may need a fire hose; possibly to hold the committee at bay.

After a relentless struggle, involving much pushing and shoving, along with a discussion regarding the lifespan of the tree, I manage to get the tree into an upright position. The committee puts down their rocks while I faint from exhaustion.

I wake up to find myself lying spread-eagled, under the tree, covered with needles. Looking down at me, the tree is smiling from limb to limb, trimmed to size and nicely decorated, thanks to my wife and kids.

With my *green belt* in Tree Wrestling, our son has been encouraging me to enter the *World Tree Wrestling* competition next December, in

Christmas Valley, Oregon. Going numerous rounds with Christmas trees has taught me several good moves. The *"Dumpster Heave"* is my favorite.

Along with the tree wrestling, I've also developed a nice tree-talk routine that our kids enjoy. I've perfected several unintelligible sounds that I like to make while attempting to put up a tree. (My wife says they're the same sounds I make when she asks me how the bedpost turned into a clothes hanger.)

One year I found the perfect tree. It was in my neighbor's living room, nicely decorated. I offered him my car in trade, but he refused. To sweeten the deal, I offered to throw in a pair of my daughter's earrings, which he could also use as road reflectors. He refused to budge. This left me no choice but to stomp out of his house in tears.

Since my neighbor squelched my attempt to obtain the perfect tree and my wife doesn't like tree wrestling in the house, I found a stress-free tree. It was a stick. I didn't even need a tree stand. I just put it in a vase with water and set it on the table. Then I topped it with an angel. People came by and asked, "Where'd you get the stick with the angel on top?"

"It's my stress-free Christmas tree," I answered. "I hope all of you find one."

I sometimes yearn for that simple Christmas of yesteryear, when I would go out with Gramps in search of the ***"Great Tree."***

He would grab his trusty axe. "Let's go out to the back forty and get us a tree," he would say. And off we would go, through rain, sleet, snow, and cold.

After walking about twenty yards, I'd ask, "Is this the back forty, Gramps?".

"No, it's up yonder," he'd answer. Then he'd point to a place much farther than you could see with the Hubble telescope.

I still remember those days as delightful times, especially if you survived the *Happy Valley Death March* to the back forty and returned with the *Great Tree.*

When our children were growing up, very few were making that long trek into the forest, staring hypothermia in the face, to find the perfect tree. They were going to tree farms or tree lots in town. I'm ashamed to admit it, but I, myself, resorted to this method.

With prices climbing every year, I not only wanted the perfect tree, I wanted the cheapest tree. "If we run out and buy the first tree we see, it will cost a *fortune*," I explained to my wife. "The key is waiting. The longer we wait, the more the price drops. If we wait long enough, we can get a great deal." I was right!

"It's just a trunk," moaned my wife.

"Look at the nice poinsettia you can set on it," I countered.

"This is not even a tree."

"Well, it's part of a tree," I answered. "It's the perfect trunk. And it's cheap. Next year we'll find a trunk with a perfect tree attached."

But the following year I encountered one of the greatest life-changing events in American history; the rise of the *ATM*, *Artificial Tree Movement*. Now I had seen it all; walking to the back forty with Gramps to cut down the *Great Tree*, to scouring tree lots in town with our kids, looking for the perfect tree, to trees that came in a box. You would take them out and assemble them right in your living room. Times were changing!

I was determined to hang on to tradition.

Shortly after artificial trees became the rage, my wife and I stopped to visit some friends during the holidays. Much to our dismay, they had shamed their name by bringing one of these trees into their home.

Although it strained our relationship, we allowed ourselves to accept several gifts, along with a plate full of cookies and fudge.

My friend said he just couldn't pass up a deal he found at an artificial tree farm. "We toured their assembly line and saw how they made the trees," he said. "Afterward, they let us make our own tree."

"Next time I'd get limbs that match," I said.

Not long thereafter, we discovered our daughter and son-in-law had gotten an artificial tree. Obviously, I was deeply hurt. *Where is the thrill of the hunt*? I thought. We once went out in search of the *Great Tree*. Now we call *QVC*, and *UPS* delivers it to our door in a box. I'm afraid we're losing the rich heritage of our past.

Not only does an artificial tree have the fragrance of the inside of a box, you have to put them together. That means they have to be taken apart after Christmas. You start missing parts.

What happens next year, when you can't find the trunk? It means **YOU** get to be the trunk, standing upright while holding a limb in each hand. Then your wife flocks you until you look as though you've been stranded outside in a blizzard for a week. To top it off, she sprays you so you'll smell like a tree. Try going to the mall like that.

It wasn't long before my wife wanted an artificial tree. "The money we spend each year on a real tree could go toward an artificial tree," she insisted.

"We had a nice tree last year," I said.

"No, we had a nice poinsettia on a stump," she answered. "I want a tree this year. If we bought an artificial tree, we wouldn't have to buy another tree."

So I priced artificial trees, and calculated that we could have one paid off by the time we were dead if we lived long enough. Then I priced artificial stumps.

My aversion to artificial trees probably comes from my childhood. Mom had an artificial tree. It was a shiny silver tree. It looked as though someone had taken a chrome hubcap, put it through a shredder, and used the remains for a tree. Every year I would ask, "Mom, where did you get that tree?"

"In the silver forest," she would answer.

It was probably where I had first spotted the elusive silver elk.

As an added attraction, she had a spotlight shining through a multi-colored disc that rotated next to the tree. As the disc rotated, the tree would change colors, from red to green to blue, and so on. If you stared at the tree long enough, you'd be hypnotized. I think that was Mom's plan. After I had stared at the tree for a while, she would lead me around the house, issuing commands…"*Make your bed*"…"*Pick up your clothes*"…"*Clean your room*"…"*Re-wire the house*"…

Anyway, I tried valiantly to keep "tradition" alive. But under intense pressure from my wife, twisting my arm, and nearly dislocating my shoulder, I finally agreed to try an artificial tree. She found the perfect tree on TV. She told me she was impressed by a new 2005 model on QVC. I told her I was more impressed by an old 1700 model I saw in the forest. Since the 1700 model wasn't for sale, I listened to the benefits of the 2005 tree.

She said the shopping channel host had the tree up in two minutes. I told my wife I was not the shopping channel host. If I was, the tree would not go up in two minutes; two hours, maybe, but not two minutes." Then she proceeded to tell me the tree would automatically light up when it was standing. "I'm sure the tree would refuse to stand for me. Trees and I have always had a rather tenuous relationship. If it *did* stand, it wouldn't light up. I would be the one 'lighting up.'"

Needless to say, the tree won. After selling both cars, we had enough money for a down payment. The tree was delivered to our front door in a large box. It arrived in time to perform for Christmas. After dragging it into the house, I sat down to catch my breath. Then I looked at the printing on the box. "Trees used to come from the back forty," I told my wife. "Now they come from Hong Kong. That's what it says on the box."

"That's further than the back forty," she answered.

"That's probably why they cost as much as a new purse," I said. "It's a lot further walk to Hong Kong."

I pulled the contents out of the box. After being satisfied that a tree was included, I looked at the directions. They were written in Chinese, probably retaliating for the leftovers I had sent them as a kid, when Mom told me they were starving in China.

To my good fortune, I spotted another set of directions in English. As I read the directions, I wondered what Gramps would have thought. "You need *directions* to put up a tree?" Then he'd grab his trusty axe and head for the back forty. "Why pay to build a tree, when you can go out to the back forty and cut one down that's already been put together, and it's **FREE!**"

Anyway, the tree came in three easy-to-assemble pieces. Shoot! It was so easy I could've assembled it in Chinese. They should have given me directions for disassembling the tree. I couldn't do it in any language. And I was speaking in several unknown tongues. If I could have taken the three pieces apart, moving the tree downstairs would have been simple, but "*simple*" and "*easy*" have never been part of my holiday plans.

I didn't want to challenge the tree while it was in one piece. The fight would have been a mismatch. I had to separate it into three pieces, so I could move it into the basement, where it would vacation until next Christmas.

It didn't take me long to realize these three easy-to-assemble parts would be extremely difficult to separate. It wouldn't be a one-person job. It would require a friend or a hammer. I looked at the directions again. Oh, there it is! *Tools required*: *friend*. So I called a friend. He was out of town for a week. When he returned, he helped me separate the three sections. Then I marched them down to the basement.

I had the same problem the following year. To my good fortune, a long, lost cousin paid us a visit shortly after Christmas, in March. I told him we'd been too busy to take down the tree.

"I'll help if you want to take it down now," he said.

I yawned and slowly answered, "I guess now is as good as any." I didn't want him to think I was getting ready to flag down a motorist for help. The two of us managed to separate the tree into its three equal sections, without incident.

Every year I had the same problem. Last year I was out of friends, so I had to use the hammer. During the process of breaking the three sections apart, a couple limbs took a mild beating. After welding the limbs back in place, the tree looked as good as new.

For next year, I've decided to leave the three sections apart, and place them side by side in the living room. We'll just decorate three small trees.

Now my wife is thinking about a new artificial tree. I'm thinking..."What! Did the tree we're still making payments on suddenly die? Did the needles turn brown and fall off? As far as I know, artificial trees cannot die."

"Why do we need a new artificial Christmas tree?" I ask.

"It's like buying a new car. They're always updating them with new features," says my wife.

"Yeah, I saw the updated prices. I think I'll look for a good, used tree; one without any body damage; with lights that still work."

Then, on the other hand, I think I'm ready to go back to a more simple time, and take my grandson on that pilgrimage to the back forty in search of the "*Great Tree*." That would be perfect.

Let's Pretend

An imagination is a marvelous thing. It will take you anywhere you'd like to go; from the warm beaches of Cancun to the ground blizzards of the Arctic. If it has taken you to the Arctic, I would check for faulty wiring.

For me, it has been a wonderful way to travel. It made school tolerable. While my body was sitting behind a desk, my mind would be exploring the world. The only downside was the fire and smoke, and debris field on my re-entry into reality. This is why I was always reluctant to return. As soon as the smoke cleared, there would be **Miss Quailbreath** glaring at me..."*Mr. Maberry, where have you been?*"

"Uh...Spring Training in Florida?"

"Did you take your schoolwork to the ballpark? Oh, no, I see you forgot and left it on your desk. Why don't you stay after school and I will give you some time to finish it."

I figured my imagination would be the only way I would see a diploma. The fact that I escaped with one in hand was considered a miracle by some of my classmates.

With all of our technology, I've often wondered if today's kids have the kind of imaginations that made our lives magical years ago.

Our grandchildren have proven they are not lacking in this area. As soon as they walk in the door of our home, they think they have entered Uncle Scrooge's vault. Then their grandmother and I will take them to a store. They imagine us with vast sums of money, to be used at their disposal, for buying anything they desire. I know they've entered Fairyland. I tell them to imagine what they would like to buy, and I'll imagine myself paying for it. Then they can imagine taking it home and playing with it.

Last night I was watching my grandson pretend he was a Transformer. I marveled at his imagination. It didn't require money. Soon his father came into the room and suggested he transform into his pajamas for bed. Brett immediately did his imitation of a five year old with an ear-piercing wail. If you've never heard the ear-piercing wail of a five year old, let me say this; it's a painful way to get your ears pierced. His performance was so good it appeared to be stark reality. I wanted to clap, but I couldn't take my hands off my ears.

When we were kids, my cousin, Lester, and I loved to pretend. Sometimes we would even pretend to be ourselves, although our parents said they preferred us being someone else. That way, if we got into trouble, they wouldn't get the blame for raising incorrigible misfits.

Even after child labor laws, much of our time was spent doing reading, writing, and math at school. There was no technology like the internet, video games, or texting. But we knew there was a world of adventure waiting for us. We just had to tap into our imagination. It was our only hope of escaping from the harsh, unrelenting world of schoolwork.

With our imaginations, we entered into an exciting world of make-believe; a world that allowed us to date the best-looking girl in school. That, alone, made an imagination worth every cent.

Gramps' ranch was the perfect setting for two young cowboys with wild and vivid imaginations. As long as we didn't shoot up the house, we were welcome to pretend.

I still love to pretend. For example, every New Year's Day I will say, "This year I'm going to get organized."

"You've still got that wild and vivid imagination," my wife will say. Of course, I'm pretending. It's a universal truth that you can't be organized when chaos (I like to call it *"Alternative Order."*) is your "calling."

Even as a child, I was not familiar with "organization." I once asked my mother about it, and she said it wasn't included in our *DNA*. I thought *DNA* meant *"Do Not Ask."* So I never mentioned it again.

Although I witnessed numerous UFO sightings growing up, encounters with organization were almost non-existent. As kids, my cousins and I would play a delightfully entertaining game called **Hide and Seek**. One of us would be given time to hide, then, at the signal, everyone else would join in the hunt; like a fox hunt without horses and hounds.

As an adult, I still enjoy a rendition of that game. It's called **Lose and Seek**. The object of the game is to use a tool, and then lay it in such a place that it will require several days to find. It's a much more difficult game than Hide and Seek.

For me, it was much easier finding kids than tools. Of course, we really weren't very smart as kids. I suspect if we'd given each other tools' names like "Screwdriver" or "Hammer," we would still be looking for each other.

I was using one of my prized screwdrivers recently. When I was finished, I laid it in such a place that it couldn't be found. Finding it would require a widespread tool hunt. After 24 hours, I called the **Missing Tools Hotline**. "I would like to file a missing tools report," I stated.

"We'll need a name," the man replied.

"Screwdriver," I answered.

"Can you give us a description?" he asked.

"Slender; nice handle; easy to work with; always shows up for work."

"We'll need a picture of your screwdriver. Also, before we organize a nationwide tool hunt and put your screwdriver on billboards, we'd like to ask you to do one thing," he said.

"I'll do anything to find my screwdriver," I answered.

"Try mowing your lawn," he suggested.

Thanks to his keen insight and timely advice, I was able to locate my screwdriver almost immediately. I quickly learned that the lawnmower is an excellent device for finding tools. Sure, you have to be alert for flying shrapnel, but you always find your tool.

I once mowed my entire yard several times in search of my favorite hammer. The yard began to look like a putting green. There was still no hammer. I became suspicious. While I was in the garage, I noticed someone had been tampering with the lid on my old, unused toolbox. Throwing the lid open, I was shocked at what I found. There, in plain sight, was my hammer. "Why isn't this in the yard," I asked my son, "in the high grass where it won't get lost?"

"Sorry, Dad," he said, "I thought I had left it in the yard, but I guess I forgot and mistakenly put it in the toolbox."

As a precaution, I put a deadbolt lock on the box. If any organized person put my tools in it, I would never find them.

Our son was usually very good about leaving things out. He was especially adept at leaving clothes strewn across his bedroom floor. His room looked like there had been a raging *"clothes blizzard."* It was a great example of "Alternative Order." Anytime I entered his room, I notified my wife. I would also carry a three day supply of food and water. Because of all the clothes, I wasn't sure of my footing. So I carried a walking stick. I used it to steady myself, and also to beat the clothes on the floor along my path. I never knew what lied beneath. Some clothes had been on the floor for so long, they had roots. They were growing. Over a period of three days, I saw a shirt go from a small to a large. One day, as I was leaving, an arm on one of his long-sleeved shirts wrapped itself around one of my legs, and wouldn't let go. I managed to escape when my wife grabbed the end of my walking stick, and pulled me to freedom.

"I could use these clothes for mulch," she said.

"Any clothes that are moving on their own, I would leave them alone."

"Okay," she said, "but I've got to get this room organized. So she brought in *Mr. Closet Organizer*. When he saw our son's room, he jumped back a couple steps. "I would tear out the closet and give him

122

more floor space," he advised. After giving it some thought, I agreed. Our son would never find a shirt hanging in the closet.

It's okay to read about highly effective, organized people as a matter of humorous reading, but don't take any "How to" books on organization as serious reading. Order will not make you happy. Sure, it makes effective, ordered people happy as they go straight to a file drawer and pull out important papers. But that isn't you. You're more comfortable looking for important documents *under your bed*, *behind a five hundred pound bookcase, in the garbage,* or *under the driver's seat in your car*. That is you. *Alternative Order* is your comfort zone. Being organized would make you a miserable wretch.

But be alert! There are people who want to organize your life; to turn make-believe into reality. Just today my own wife, forgetting about past failures, made another attempt to bring order into my life. She bought me a monthly planner. It was one that I didn't have, so I put it with my collection. For those who collect them, it is a very nice gift. I have attended several monthly planner trade shows, where people from all across the United States meet to display and trade planners. It's very much like a stamp show. If you trade, always make sure there is no writing inside. That devalues them. My greatest find was a monthly planner on a stone tablet.

She also told me about someone in our area who could come in and organize our garage. "They will create storage where there is no storage," she said.

"Frankly, I don't know what's so great about that," I told her. "I've done the same thing for years, and it was free!"

In our office, my wife loves everything organized nicely in a file folder. That's probably why I can never find anything. Having a preference for *Alternative Order*, I like the *"pocket"* file. This is where I keep important notes and other critical information. Important notes and other critical information mean anything I consider humorous that could go into a hardly-sought-after book.

According to my teachers, who were willing to speak only on condition of anonymity, I never took notes in school. I'm sure this was because I found very little humor in algebra, biology and woodshop. I also had to deal with more important matters, like trying to remember where I was supposed to meet my wandering mind after school.

Today I am a prolific note taker, writing notes on any scrap of paper I can find; old receipts, corners of newspapers, napkins, legal documents....These are not just any notes. These are important notes; notes that could go into a highly disclaimed book.

They are stored in my *"pocket"* file, where they remain until it looks as though I'm carrying a water bottle in each pocket.

Occasionally, I think I've misplaced them, so I'll ask my wife, "Connie, have you seen my notes?"

"Here they are," she says, as she hands me a little white paper ball.

Once again, I have to remind myself to get my notes into a safe place before she starts washing my clothes.

I once thought I could rescue some of my hardly-sought-after material by throwing several little white paper balls into the dryer. I don't need to tell you how that worked. As soon as I opened the dryer door, I was staring at the remnants of a paper blizzard.

"Maybe if you run outside to the dryer vent, you can hear some laughs coming out," said my wife.

"That's why you need to get rid of those crazy scraps of paper," ranted Lester. "You can't sit outside all night with your ear to the vent. People will start asking questions."

"What do you suggest?" I asked.

"Use my method," he said. "Write notes on your hands and arms."

"I don't want to look like the front page of the local paper, "I answered. "Besides, every time you go to the library, people ask to check you out for two weeks. And the librarian wants to file one of your arms for future reference."

Lester said it was a small price to pay for eliminating the potential of losing valuable information.

I thought Lester was a lone steely in a sea of marbles until my good friend and teacher, Tommy Hawk, told me his students did the same thing. "I offer them paper, but they prefer keeping all their notes on their hands and arms. I guess it's good to have students who are open books."

Personally, I don't want to be an open book. I'm not comfortable having people ask, "*Can I look at the back of your hand?* I think it has the directions to my hotel."..."*Remember to look under your arm. You have a dinner appointment at 6.*"..."*I love what you said on your elbow. It was hysterical.*"..."*That was a very funny story on your wrist.*"..."*If you hold your arm still, I can finish reading.*"

I think I'll stay with my pocket files.

Unless you get gene therapy, don't try to be someone you're not. Be yourself. If you are always pulling your hair out, looking for a critical document that you needed yesterday, embrace it.

I love to watch people pretend; trying to get organized when their world is *Alternative Order*. Seeing them in action is not a pretty sight. If they think you're stopping by their house for a visit, they fly into action: flinging, stuffing, piling, throwing, and sweeping. By the time you arrive, their closets are bulging, and they have swept so much under the rug, their living room looks like a national landmark. "Oh, the '***Indian Mounds***,'" you marvel. "I didn't realize they were so close."

If you are not organized, don't worry about it. Remember, it has taken you years to get where you are. It would take a revolution, not a resolution, to get organized. Then you wouldn't be happy; no hardhat area for falling boxes; no newspaper avalanche control; no narrow pathways to circumnavigate. Organization would ruin your life.

I think there should be a seminar on "***How to Achieve Optimum Chaos, I mean 'Alternative Order', in your Life.***" I would be more than willing to teach the class, if I could find my notes. I know they're here somewhere. Let me check my pockets.

If you still want to be organized, let's pretend.

Here Comes Christmas!

Time is an odd thing. When you're young, you almost have to push it along. This is especially true if you're waiting for a dog to magically appear on your doorstep, math to become extinct, or Christmas to arrive before you run out of "**good**." When you're older, time goes by so fast it spins you around like a top. This is why older people have problems with vertigo; time is passing too fast. I'm sure it's also the reason Christmas arrives long before I've done my shopping.

As a young boy, I would wait several years for it to appear. Now it won't leave me alone. It's always sneaking up on me. I can't get through Thanksgiving dinner without Christmas staring at me through the window. I would recognize that stare anywhere. I try not to look, but the kids shout, "Hey! Isn't that Christmas watching us?"

"It's just reminding me that it's nearby, and that I need to awaken from my pre-Christmas slumber," I answer.

My anxiety will soon be running on all six cylinders, as I rush out the door to do my last minute shopping. I call it the Christmas body-slam.

I'm convinced all of this is due to the earth slipping off its axis, although my wife insists that I'm the one who has slipped off his axis as I've been spinning out of control for some time.

Seriously, I'm the epitome of calm...until the Christmas season. Okay, I may slip off my axis when I'm driving in Seattle. But everyone is off their axis in that traffic.

The real challenge begins with the holidays. The other day I went to do some last minute shopping. I made several loops around the mall parking lot, without success. I could feel myself beginning to slip. Then I tapped the parking space locator app on my phone. It said there was a space available in western Kansas. I pulled myself back onto my axis and went home to look for something online.

The Christmas season is my greatest challenge. It's not that I don't enjoy being trampled by hordes of shoppers, buying a parked car so I will have a parking space, or using conflict resolution to keep my place in line at checkout. It's the fact that I add another disorder to my cart...Shopping Anxiety Disorder. Now I can check out. The Christmas season is all the anxiety I need.

When I go to the mall, I'm not hard to spot. I'm the one standing there paralyzed, with a wild-eyed, desperate look. I prefer shopping at a hospital gift shop, so I will be close to help. I have no trouble buying for our cat, but buying for people causes anxiety. There are so many decisions. Will it fit? Will it match? Is it the right color? Will they like it? And I'm just talking about a refrigerator magnet! Shopping would be so much easier if I could just go out and buy everyone a can of Friskies.

Last Christmas, while all the relatives had gathered at my in-laws for a festive evening and gift exchange, I was following my normal schedule; searching frantically for that special, unforgettable gift. It was an exercise in futility. "I'm sorry," said the clerk. "You just missed our perfect last-minute gift sale." I stopped exercising long enough to catch my breath, but it fled before I could catch it. My anxiety level was bubbling at peak capacity. I considered my options. "Panic" looked like a good one. Then I spotted a gift. Not the perfect gift, but something unusual. I purchased the gift and rushed back to the house, arriving in a dead heat with Santa, just before gifts were exchanged.

We all took turns opening our presents. When it was my wife's turn, she ripped off the wrapping paper in eager anticipation. When she saw my gift, she was speechless. After a moment of silence, she asked, "What is it?"

"It's one of those robotic vacuum cleaners that hover over the floor. It works by itself. You don't have to touch it. It even has a special *"mouse sensor app."* When it senses a mouse nearby, an alarm goes off. Then it goes after the mouse. But you have to make sure the "suction adjustment" setting is in the right position. If it's set too high, this thing can suck a door off its hinges, going for a mouse. If it's working properly, it can suck up a generation of mice in an afternoon.

"Very romantic," she answered.

Okay, it may not have been that special, but it was certainly unforgettable. I think this is why my mother would buy her own gift, along with a nice card, and say it was from me. She didn't trust my gifts.

This year my wife invited me to join her in the ultimate shopping experience, *"Black Friday."* It marks the beginning of the Christmas shopping season. This shopping frenzy the day after Thanksgiving is a test of endurance. Millions of wild-eyed *"Black Friday"* fanatics rush out of their homes in the middle of the night, descending on stores like a swarm of crazed locusts. Their goal: To be the first in line when the stores open. It's an event that will bring you to your knees, as people climb up your back so they can use your shoulders as a springboard to jump over others in front of you. If you are looking for peace on earth, this is not it. If you want peace, lock yourself in the closet.

My wife made it clear I wouldn't be required to do any shopping. I could just go for the writing material. So a week before the big event, I met with my personal trainer for a vigorous workout; bobbing and weaving; dancing and darting around the shopping carts he was shoving at me. This helps me adjust to the speed and direction of the cart. This way I can time my moves to avoid being struck and, possibly, pinned under a militant cart.

The morning after Thanksgiving, I got up early and turned on the TV, hoping to get the latest news on the *"Black Friday"* shopping wars.

Most stores were reporting stop and go in their aisles, while others reported pushing and shoving, with limited visibility due to overcrowding. There were several reports of "Aisle Rage." Other than a lone smack down, there were no other confirmed injuries. There had been a cart attack on aisle three at one store. Another store was reporting a mild skirmish on aisle seven. One department store had to close down two aisles after a multiple cart pileup. I wanted to go back to bed and hide under the covers. I thought, *"This could be payback for last year's vacuum with the mouse app!"*

"Don't believe what you see on TV," said my wife. "It's much worse."

"Forget the covers," I thought. *"I'm getting **under** the bed."*

Before I could find out who won the war, my wife had pulled me out from under the bed, and we were off to Walmart. I was headed into the center of the storm. I soon found myself in Walmart's version of the "Corn Maze." But, instead of weaving your way through cornstalks, you're weaving your way through shopping carts.

Drivers have to dodge carts that have been positioned randomly throughout the parking lot by patrons who choose not to be identified. The objective is to avoid being hit by an errant cart, or surrounded by militant carts. Drivers must also be aware of other drivers who are working their way through the "Cart Maze."

This is not for the faint of heart. For safety reasons, anyone entering the "Maze" should be in good health, and free from high blood pressure, heart, back or neck problems, motion sickness, nervous disorders, or other conditions that could be aggravated by the "Maze." Check with your family doctor to see if this "Maze" is right for you.

Expectant mothers and those who have P.A.D. (Parking Anxiety Disorder) should stay home.

The "Maze" tests a driver's alertness, reaction time, and ability to refrain from shouting at unmanned carts, and imaginary people.

The "Maze" is being considered as a future Olympic event, called Extreme Parking.

One gentleman didn't read the rules about remaining in your car until you were parked. He had jumped out, shoved one cart out of the way, and was yelling at anyone grasping a cart handle to return it to the cart stall immediately, or they could forget Santa. I guess there is always going to be one poor sport.

I didn't fare too well, myself. I jumped a median and ran over some shrubs in an attempt to squeeze between carts, and park the car. I was disqualified, and had to give my keys to a Walmart valet, who parked the car for me.

Connie and I made our way into the store. After dodging numerous carts and watching two men compete in a tug-of-war for a television, I looked for a bed to hide under. I had to resign myself to a bench where I could sit and watch the action. While I was sitting, Connie did some Rugby shopping. In this event, you grab your gift and run for the cashier. Several other shoppers grab on to you as you're running, and try to dislodge the gift. You try to remain on your feet, looking for a friend to hand off to, so they can carry it on to the cashier. Training with an Australian Football team is a big plus for this competition.

On our way home, Connie lost control of the steering wheel, and the car veered into a mall. As she explained it, "Sometimes things happen that are completely out of your control."

"Just one of those involuntary reflexes," I answered.

As we entered the shopping abyss, my anxiety began to bubble. Connie directed me to a Starbucks, where I enjoyed a cup of coffee and a nice roll someone had left in a sack on the counter. Combining it with a sports page had a nice calming effect on my disorder.

Connie found herself in the "American Girl" store; a very dangerous place to find yourself. If you have a granddaughter, you know "American Girl." If you have a granddaughter and DON'T know "American Girl," you're deceased.

By the time my wife came out, I was on my third cup of coffee, had read the sports pages of several major papers, and was now nervously pacing the mall, knowing that it was cheaper delivering a real baby, than buying an "American Girl" doll.

When I saw her walk out of the store carrying a bag, my heart started to make a run for my mouth. But she quickly informed me it wasn't a doll, just several hundred dollars' worth of clothes. My heart made another run for my mouth. I swallowed hard to get it back into place.

After several more nerve-wracking hours, it was time to go home for some rest, and prepare myself for Christmas Eve, when I would rush out of the house just before the stores closed, in search of the perfect gift. I wondered what gift cards would be available.

I knew Christmas would soon be gone, leaving as quickly as it had come. But I also knew there was another Christmas lurking around the corner. I was just hoping it would quit staring at me through the window.

Shopping Disorders and the Mall Spirit

Because of my own struggles with **S.A.D.**, *Shopping Anxiety Disorder*, I've become extremely interested in others who struggle with shopping maladies; they provide great writing material.

Not long ago I spotted an article on **"RTD,"** *Retail Therapy Disease*, commonly known as *"**Comfort Shopping**."* I got excited. I had never experienced any comfort in shopping. I thought this article might help me deal with my shopping anxieties. Instead, the article explained the reasons some women are compulsive shoppers. It also suggested a possible cure.

Not long after I read the article, I received a call from my friend, Fred. His wife had just been diagnosed with **"RTD."** She was apparently exposed through contact with her daughter-in-law. The doctor said she had a highly aggressive form of "comfort shopping," although Fred didn't find much comfort in it. There was the distinct possibility it might not be curable.

"I should have suspected a problem at Christmas, when she asked for a personalized shopping cart with her name engraved on the handle," moaned Fred. "Now it seems like they spend every moment together," he went on.

I felt terrible for Fred; losing his wife's love to a shopping cart.

Apparently, women deal with their stresses by shopping. They comfort shop when they're anxious, when work is going badly, when they're fighting with their spouse, or when they're concerned about the drought in southern Chile.

"That explains why she's been unable to sleep at night, "said Fred, excitedly. "She's been concerned about the drought in southern Chile."

"Are you sure your wife isn't under duress because she thought she married you, but discovered too late that she had really married soccer...baseball...football...and assorted other sports?"

"No, I'm sure it's the drought," answered Fred.

I told him about the article and explained that help was available. "Scientists have discovered a drug that may curb her compulsive desire to shop," I said. "They've tried the drug on seven patients and all seven have shown a dramatic reduction in the urge to shop."

"It must have caused paralysis," answered Fred, with a hint of skepticism.

"No, I'm serious," I continued.

"I'm sure my wife's immune system would resist it," he insisted. "The doctor told me her case is the worst he's ever seen. She just left today on a seven day mall tour. If they don't get some rain soon in southern Chile, my pocketbook will be facing a severe drought."

After his wife had returned from her mall tour with a pocketbook as dry as southern Chile, she agreed to try the drug.

After a couple of weeks, I called. "How did it work?" I asked.

"I thought it was great," answered Fred. "We were out shopping, and she walked right by a 75% off sale. She just yawned and said she needed to get home so she could re-plumb the house."

"It must be working," I said.

"It was until it wore off," Fred continued. "Now she's gone on a twelve-day hunt for a trophy chair. I had to pay a plumber to come in and finish her job."

I am happy to report that very few men are afflicted with this disease. Just hearing the "**S**" word will cause most men to experience symptoms of extreme fatigue, light-headedness and nausea, with the need to lie down in front of the television. A good ballgame will usually clear up these symptoms and lead to a full recovery. A little fishing or hunting can also speed up the recovery. I've even known some who found that a simple round of golf was a perfect cure. My cousin, Skeeter, thought kayaking the narrows would clear up his symptoms, but he barely survived the experience. "Next time I'll use the kayak," he said. The shopping cart was recovered several miles downstream.

Although the drug for curing "**RTD**" has been proven effective, there are other preventive measures a person can take to avoid using the drug.

Personally, I prefer going to the mall when the stores are closed. Mall walking in the morning, before the stores open, is a perfect time, but even that can be fraught with peril. Just recently, I witnessed the abduction of a totally innocent mall walker. She was walking along briskly, minding her own business and getting her exercise for the day when, without warning, a curtain on one of the stores opened up and she mysteriously disappeared. Thirty minutes later she reappeared, apparently unharmed, but loaded down with an armful of packages. It was an eerie experience to witness. I had heard of the *Mall Spirit*, but this was the first time I had seen it in action. I called Fred. "Maybe your wife is just under the control of the *Mall Spirit*," I said.

"It's very possible," answered Fred. "I know it's not my Spirit. Last week she woke up in the middle of the night, saying a voice kept telling her the drought in southern Chile was getting worse. I tried to tell her it was my voice, telling her our pocketbook was drying up. She refused to believe me."

"It must be the *Mall Spirit*," I said.

I learned that if you're not forever vigilant, the *Mall Spirit* can catch you by surprise, and it's not easy getting out of its grasp.

Just recently, my wife and a friend were preparing to go to the mall...just the usual routine: some long distance running, a little weightlifting, qualifying time trials on the shopping cart obstacle course in the Wal-Mart parking lot---the graveyard for just-used shopping carts; typical preparation for holiday shopping.

"Would you like to go with us?" Connie asked.

"I'd feel safer bounding through the forest with a large rack and white tail during hunting season," I answered.

"I'll buy you a new tie if you promise not to snag it on the brush as you're bounding through the forest," she went on.

Being good-natured and thinking I could spend my time sleeping...I mean, reading at the bookstore, I went along for the ride. It began just as I had planned. I was sitting in a large, soft leather chair enjoying a good book. Realizing I was in my element, dozing in a comfortable chair with a good book covering my face, Connie walked over and said, "Wake, come and look at this pair of pants. I think you would like them." This is when I could sense the *Mall Spirit* nearby. With little warning, my time of relaxation was about to spiral out of control into the black hole of shopping. I was about to be caught in the web of the Mall Spirit.

Before long I had a pair of pants, shoes, shirt, belt, and tanning lotion, although I think the tanning lotion was for the *Mall Spirit*. It happened so quickly I had no time to react. My wife said it was a bargain. I agreed. I never question a bargain. I crossed that line once. I didn't like what I saw, so I jumped back behind the line. Afterwards, my wife helped me see how we were actually making money. If it's 50% off, she takes the 50% she saves and buys the gift. The other half she pockets. The more she buys, the more we save. So I got a loan to invest in more 50% off sales. It was a great little money-maker.

Several days after returning home from the black hole of shopping, Connie was off again on another money-making venture at the mall.

135

She hadn't been gone long, when my irascible cousin, Lester, stopped by for a visit. He walked in just as I was catching my breath. "It looks like you just finished running a marathon," he said.

"No, I was just wrestling with that age-old question. What do I get my wife for her birthday? Just when I thought I had the question pinned down, it got up and knocked the wind out of me."

"I can see why you're huffing and puffing," said Lester. "It's a question that's turned many strong, self-made men into blathering idiots. For weasels like us, it's even more challenging."

"What do you get a woman who has every magnet in the world?" I asked Lester. "Her jewelry box is overflowing, and the magnets are two-deep on the refrigerator."

"Maybe go three-deep?" quizzed Lester.

When Connie returned later that night I approached her with rare bluntness. "What would you like for your birthday?" I asked.

"I'd love anything," she answered. "Remember, it's the thought that counts."

So I thought about it. It wasn't long before I realized I was getting low on thoughts. I wasn't sure how many were still in stock. I might have to resort to an actual gift. I started getting nervous twitches. A skin rash was beginning to appear. My anxiety level was climbing toward overload. I looked around the house for my stick, thinking I might round up a wild boar. I went outside for some fresh air. Just when my thoughts were running on fumes, a bright light appeared in the sky. It had to be the *Mall Spirit*. I followed the bright light. It led me to a car dealership that was offering free balloons and hot dogs to anyone who would listen to a sales pitch. I listened to the sales pitch. Then I went home. "Happy Birthday," I said, handing Connie a hot dog and nice balloon.

"How thoughtful," she replied.

"I decided you had enough magnets."

With my **S.A.D.**, it was nice to get a little help from the *Mall Spirit.*

The Jaws of Winter

I was just sitting outside on the deck, having my coffee, and contemplating summer's departure. "I hate it when summer leaves so quickly," I mentioned to my wife. "I'm not ready for those long, dark, and dangerous days of winter."

"What are you moaning about?" she asked. "It's June!"

"I know, but winter isn't far off," I said, looking at my watch.

I was still having flashbacks of last winter, when I was driving home on 50 miles of snow-covered roads. I had questioned the wisdom of driving home that night. But I finally threw caution to the wind. Shoot! As soon as I threw it, I knew it was a mistake. Anyway, I began the drive home, making sure to follow the advice my Grandpa had given me years before; always wear clean underwear, and go with the slide. I thought, "What if I don't like where the slide is going? Does that mean I need an extra set of underwear?"

This particular night, my car was sliding in all directions. I didn't like any of them. And I spoke to the car about it. Completely ignoring my concerns, the car then did several fish tails, a 360 spin-around, a couple figure 8's, along with some other moves I had never seen. I finally let the car drive on its own, since it wasn't letting me drive. While it was driving, I got out my camera and took some great close-up shots of drivers in the other cars screaming as my car went by. On two separate occasions, I saw passengers jump into the back seat.

My car finally managed to point itself in the right direction. Then it let me drive again. When I arrived home, I stopped at the top of our snow-covered driveway and parked the car. Going down the driveway would mean a harrowing ride down to the lower forty and, possibly, into Canada, with a cow for a hood ornament. Of course, the other cows would probably give me a standing ovation.

While I sat in the car at the top of the driveway, I surveyed the best path to the house; a path that would allow me to remain on my feet the entire distance. I don't like sliding out of control on ice and snow, especially when I'm on foot. I finally spotted a path I liked. Getting out of the car, I gingerly maneuvered across the ice in the driveway. Suddenly, my feet went up and the rest of my body went down. I had chosen the wrong path. I was sliding down our driveway, cleverly disguised as a bobsled. I was headed for the garage. It was fortunate that I was holding the garage door opener in one hand, and was able to open the door as I was sliding its way. When I arrived in the garage, I heard Connie say, "Don't forget to shut the garage door and turn off your engine." I was just hoping I had enough gas in the engine to get into the house.

The other day I saw an ad that pictured the four seasons. It posed the question, "Which season makes you feel most at ease?" Let's see…do I feel more at ease reading a book in my lounge chair on the deck in the warm sun, or do I feel more at ease tip-toeing across the ice and snow, like it's a high wire act, hoping I don't slip and fall to my death. Okay, I'll take the lounge chair in the warm sun.

Unlike summer, when the days fly by so fast, you don't have time to put your boat in the water (although not having a boat can add to the problem), winter is filled with long, dreary days of darkness. It brings time to a near standstill. There is very little movement. My wife says she notices the same thing when she asks me to take out the garbage; there's very little movement. Anyway, after peering into the darkness for days and weeks, I gradually degenerate into a formless mass of jelly. My wife looks for me, and there I am, puddled up on the floor. She believes I may have a mild form of **Seasonal Affective Disorder**, a condition that robs a person of their cheery outlook when they spend the winter locked in a dark closet, or in Alaska. And you don't want to be locked in Alaska all winter.

Those who suffer from **S.A.D.** often feel like winter days are twice as long as those during the summer. I, myself, have seen some winter days that equaled, at least, three days of summer.

My good friend, Ozzie, has been struggling with the disorder for years. I think he's in the final stages.

S.A.D. is caused by a lack of sunlight. So Ozzie has been experimenting with one of those special lights in a box. You know, light therapy. It mimics sunlight. He says the light has really helped. It may keep his disorder from spreading beyond the final stages, when you turn into amoeba.

If you suffer from this disorder, the first thing you should do is eat all the chocolate in the house. This will keep you functioning until you can find a project that will get your mind off the long days of drear. Ozzie told me this plan may be better than the light.

Now he has found the perfect project. I stopped by to check it out. He had a large table covered with beautiful fall leaves. I thought he was starting a collection. "No," he said, "I'm going green."

"What do you mean, you're 'going green.'"

"That's what I said. I'm going to paint these leaves green."

"You're kidding!"

"No! Then I'm going to put them back on that tree right there."

"What! You can't put leaves back on a tree."

"Yes, I can! I have a hot glue gun."

"You've got to be kidding!"

"No! Then I'm going to get my light therapy box and heat lamp, and put them next to my hammock so I can lie down and read, just like I do in the summer."

"I've never seen you read in a hammock! You don't even own a hammock!"

"I know, but I'm going to buy one."

"Maybe you should consider Arizona. You wouldn't have to watch out for dripping glue and falling leaves, while you're reading."

Like Ozzie, coping with **Seasonal Affective Disorder** causes people to resort to extreme measures. Some will even resort to exercise. I don't believe I would go to that extreme. I prefer complaining until my wife has stockpiled enough chocolate for several winters.

For the more sensible, staying busy with activities is a great cure for the doldrums. Something you might want to consider is the annual *Fruitcake Toss* competition. It's held on the first Saturday of January in Manitou Springs, Colorado. This is a great way to get your mind off the dark and drear. It's also an opportunity to get rid of that fruitcake you've been using as a doorstop. If you have already marked your calendar, booked your hotel, and are preparing for next year's Fruitcake Toss competition, there are some things you need to know. First, always keep an eye on the sky…for flying fruitcakes. They are thrown, catapulted, and cannoned, using various inventive means. I have seen some of these inventive means. This is why I watch the competition on television in my hotel room in Denver. Just kidding! But, seriously, you need to be alert! A frozen fruitcake shot out of a cannon can shorten your smile and loosen your vocabulary if you are hit in the face.

If you choose to participate, there are rules you will have to follow. Here they are: First, you are expected to bring your own Fruitcake. If you forget, and leave your fruitcake at home on your recliner, where you've been using it as a headrest, don't worry. You can rent a fruitcake at the competition for a dollar. If you have your own fruitcake, it will be inspected by the "Fruitcake Toss Tech Inspectors." This is done to make sure there is nothing in the fruitcake that will hurt someone who might be hit in the head while it's flying on auto pilot.

There are several events. One is the *Distance Competition*. This is where you hurl a 2 pound fruitcake as far as possible. The distance is measured from the point it's thrown, to its final resting place; not where it first hits the ground. So, if you make your fruitcake in the shape of a soccer ball, you have a good chance of winning the competition.

Catch the Fruitcake is another competitive event. Here you have to catch a fruitcake that has been hurled by your device. The fruitcake cannot weigh more than one pound. This is so you don't get hurt. If your fruitcake is shot from a Cannon, it will arrive quickly. This is why it cannot weigh more than a pound. You don't want to be drilled by an overweight fruitcake. The winner is the one who catches the most fruitcakes in a given amount of time. If you are trying to catch a frozen fruitcake, I would look for a game of Scrabble.

Another competitive event is *Accuracy with Targets*. No, you aren't the target. But it's an event that will test your throwing accuracy. So you might want to get together with a friend and practice playing long toss with a fruitcake.

As you can see, January can be a fun month. It provides activities that will help you forget that spring is light years away. And you don't have to go to Manitou Springs to have fun. You can build your own fruitcake fort at a local park, and have the Fruitcake Wars. Just remember to clean up the debris before you leave the park.

The opportunities for fun in January are endless. So enjoy the month, and don't forget the 24th. That's Belly Laugh Day. And we can always use one of those; it promotes good health.

I can almost feel the Jaws of Winter loosening its grip.

Christmas Décor Showdown

I was out for a drive recently, when I noticed a bumper sticker on the car in front of me. As I got closer, I could see **P-E-A-C-E** in big red letters. I laughed. It was obvious this person had never dealt with Christmas lights.

Having spent years dealing with them, I can tell you this; as soon as you take them out of their box, you can forget about peace. I learned this early in my childhood.

Being the only child in our home, it was my job to string Christmas lights along the eaves. It would begin with the ceremonial untangling of the lights. During the untangling, I would become entangled. At the same time, Mom would plug in the lights and discover a short. People would drive by and watch the *"Dance of a Thousand Lights."*

Christmas lights have their place...tucked away in the far reaches of the attic. If they would stay there, we could give peace a chance.

But come December, I hear clamoring. It's my wife. "Honey, it's time to hang the lights." Being Christmas, I attempt to exhibit good cheer, but it always ends when I pull the lights out of the box. "Leave us in here, where it's warm," they'll say. "We don't like hanging out in the cold."

"I'm here on orders from the General, my wife," I counter, "So come with me."

I used to think I could reason with Christmas lights, but that was before I realized they were on a mission to destroy my life.

This past Christmas they were especially disagreeable. As soon as I had gotten them out of the box and began strangling...I mean untangling them, a shouting match erupted, followed by a lot of pushing and shoving. The neighbors called the police to come and separate us. I was certain they would cite the lights for assault and battery, and throw them in the back of their car. But they just seemed amused that the lights had transformed me into a living Christmas tree.

"If you stand by the porch, we're certain you'll get a canned food donation," they said, laughing merrily, as they drove away.

I was left to fend for myself.

"No justice," I muttered.

The lights have a much better relationship with my wife. They untangle themselves before she takes them out of the box. Then she plugs them in and they lie there, smiling and shining brightly. Why can't I enjoy that kind of relationship?

When the lights are ready, she wants me to hang them from the eaves. I find more joy hanging my shirts on doorknobs.

Before I can take off my shirt and hang it on a doorknob, Connie is back in the attic. "I think we're missing some lights," she yells.

"Those lights rode with me to the shooting range," I answer. "They got spooked by Fred."

"What do you mean...'they got spooked by Fred?'"

"Yeah, Fred was shooting up his Christmas lights, so our lights disappeared. I tried calling them before I left, but they refused to come out of hiding."

"That's a likely story."

"Huh?"

"Well, I'm going to go out and buy more lights."

"Wait! I'll go with you; I need to buy more doorknobs."

"If you keep putting up doorknobs, I won't have any more room for hanging my pictures."

"I get more respect from doorknobs. And shirts look so nice hanging on them. Besides, you can have the entire closet to yourself, and we won't have to add on. I can lay my slacks over the back of a chair."

"That means you'll have to go out and buy more chairs," said Connie.

"That's okay. Next Christmas, we can have an open house," I answered. "And give tours...'Look at the nice shirts hanging on those doorknobs, and what a great-looking pair of slacks on the back of that chair.'"

"What about the pants lying on the floor?"

"We could decorate them with lights. That should guarantee us enough canned food donations to survive the winter."

Next to hanging shirts on doorknobs, I enjoy watching the neighbors decorate for Christmas.

On occasion, I will even lend a helping hand..."Hang on to that eave, Norm, and I'll get a ladder so you'll have something to stand on."

"Why can't you hang lights from the eaves, like Norm?" asked Connie.

"Because Norm is using my ladder; besides, the lights refuse to leave their warm box."

"I'm sure they would be more cooperative if you would quit threatening to leave them hanging all winter. And, no, they don't want to ride with you to the shooting range."

Wanting to please my wife and have some dinner, I agreed to string the lights. I managed to remove them from the box without incident. Then I walked over to Norm's. "Sorry, Norm, but I need my ladder." I tried to ignore his screams as I carried the ladder around the house.

I quickly fastened the lights to the eaves. They refused to shine.

"Why don't you try this new device?" asked my wife. "It's called a **Light String Saver**. You can test the lights to see which bulbs aren't working."

"I just plugged in the lights. I don't need a 'Light String Saver' to tell me none of them are working."

"But one bulb may be the reason they're not shining," Connie continued.

In theory, one bulb is the culprit in keeping 67 other bulbs from shining brightly. This is just theory. In reality, none of the 67 bulbs work, and they're not planning on working, but taking each one out and testing it gives you something to occupy your time while you're waiting for the return of summer.

Years ago, Christmas lights were made to last. That was before the "*Christmas light elves*." Today's lights are made to last until you remove them from their box. This is because they are sensitive to touch...as soon as you touch them, they quit working. Try plugging them in and you will get a cough, sputter, and a couple flickers; then their done. It's off to the store for more lights.

This is what the *Christmas light elves* want to see; you running to the store for more lights. This is why most of them have retired to Rarotonga in the Cook Islands. They don't care if it looks like you have half a tree, when you turn on the lights; or that one out of every five bulbs work on your lights along the eaves.

Lights will test your relationship with Christmas. If you put your lights on the tree, only to find that half of them don't work, be very careful not to make any quick movements, like ripping them off the tree. This upsets the lights that are shining, and now you have darkness.

You will have more success if you handle your lights like a newborn baby. If they short out, it's their way of spitting up on you. Remember, if they do go out, you will have to find the bulb that is causing the problem. Good luck. Hopefully you will find it before

Christmas. **A word of caution**: Always let the bulbs cool before testing them. Never check a bulb by pressing it against your lips. That is stupid. A hot bulb will light you up like a Christmas tree and, for the next two weeks, your lips will look like you're blowing bubbles. And you will talk funny.

If you're looking for peace during the holidays, leave the lights in the box. Just pull the cord out and plug them in. That's what I do. People enjoy driving by to see my flashing boxes.

I once had lights shine for an entire Christmas season. I became suspicious. I knew they were planning something. The following Christmas I aroused them from their slumber. What did I find; lights that were worse than tangled fishing line! How did that happen? Who knows? The lights weren't talking. But I could hear them laughing. After a couple days, I was able to untangle the lights. Then I discovered they wouldn't shine. This is what they were planning. This is their method of torture. Don't stomp on them. Lights have great memories. Besides, you don't want the lights AND your wife against you.

For years, I was certain we had militant mice destroying our lights, seeking revenge for some relatives we refused to take in. But after talking to Christmas light scientists, I discovered that this is a universal problem. It's called the "**Law of the Christmas Lights**." Whatever shines brightly this year must short out before next Christmas. It's more certain than the **Law of Gravity**. We can put a man on the moon, but we can't get the lights to work. This is why we can put "*light elves*" in Rarotonga.

Some Christmas I would like to sit down at the bargaining table and sign a peace accord, but with a mind of their own I doubt if the lights would agree to it. Besides, the elves need spending money.

On one of her trips to the store for more lights, my wife returned with a large box which held inflatable Christmas characters. "Since we had nothing in the yard, I thought we could add this to our display of nothing," she said.

I had a flashback; then staggered backwards, like I had just received a glancing blow to the head. "I remember this picture as a kid," I said fearfully. "I remember Mom wanting more than lights. She wanted a full nativity scene, with carved, wooden, life-sized figures of the wise men, Mary and Joseph, sheep, cattle, and a cast of thousands. I had to convince her to save the cast of thousands for the Red Sea crossing, hopefully after I had left home, and wouldn't have to direct traffic."

"No, no; this will be nothing like your childhood experience," insisted Connie.

As soon as I started opening the box, I knew we were headed for trouble. "This one is going to apply to the '*Box Law*,'" I said.

"What's the '*Box Law*'?" Connie asked.

"What comes out of the original box will only go back into a box twice its size," I answered. As soon as something is removed from a box, alien powers cause the contents to grow. It's just part of the *Christmas Twilight Zone*."

Nevertheless, I finally got our inflatable blown up, which left me exhausted and out of breath. Then I saw the cord and realized I could have plugged it in and achieved the same result. I also learned that you don't just blow up an inflatable and seal the hole with a plug. For them to stay upright, you have to keep the fan running.

Nearby, they actually have a *Deflated Inflatables* tour where you can drive around looking at inflatables lying in people's yards. The home owners found it was too costly to keep the fans running. Some tried to keep them up manually. If you look closely, you may see a few deflated homeowners lying in their yard.

Every year we love to drive around with the kids, enjoying our local Parade of Lights, but one year we decided to try a new approach. We drove around admiring the homes with no lights. We called it Scrooge's *Parade of Darkness*.

"Look! There's a nice home with no lights."

"Grandpa, shine the lights on that house. I can't quite see it."

"Did a can of soup just hit the car?"

Bah, Humbug! This may catch on.

This past Christmas, while driving home and enjoying our local Trail of Lights (rush hour after dark), I was inspired to add to the

Christmas spirit. I came up with the idea of flashing red and blue headlights. I thought they were starting to catch on when I saw someone behind me with flashing red and blue lights, only his were on top of his car. After discussing our lights, I agreed to drop out of the competition. In keeping with the Christmas spirit, I complimented him on his lights, and we both enjoyed the holidays.

Important Dates
and
The Perfect Gift

I was standing in the checkout line of our local grocery one evening, when I noticed a large throng of men, possibly numbering in the hundreds, gathered at the card rack. "What's going on?" I asked the clerk.

"Tomorrow is **Mother's Day**," she answered.

I knew there was something I had forgotten! It had been in the back of my mind, but it was so far back that my memory was late arriving. I immediately dropped everything and ran to join the masses.

Wiping away a nervous sweat, I realized there were no more Mother's Day cards. That meant I would have to buy a get well card and re-write it to fit the occasion. Then I thought...*I might need a get well card for myself, maybe even a sympathy card.* I grabbed several cards, along with a bottle of whiteout, and went to find the perfect gift. My choices were wilted flowers or stale chocolates. I settled for the cards and whiteout.

Then I heard the clerk paging me. "Would the gentleman running through the store with the glazed look please return to register three and pick up the items you dropped? They are blocking the aisle."

With a calendar filled with special occasions, and more waiting to be added, I learned quickly the purpose of marriage.   It's not to be fruitful and multiply.   It's to have a wife who will remind you of important dates..."I hope you haven't forgotten that tomorrow is our anniversary."

"Shoot, I thought it was **Dead Fly Day**. *Just kidding*! How could I forget our anniversary?" I'd better see if my life insurance is paid up.

Occasionally a man will stumble upon an important date without being reminded..."Oh! Tomorrow is the beginning of fishing season! My memory must have made a temporary comeback."

When I do get an important date in my sights, it's usually behind me. Just the other day, while driving to work, I looked up, and there, in my rear view mirror, was an important date. It was tailgating me. I hate tailgaters. So I tried to outrun it. It wouldn't back off. I finally pulled off the road and stopped. It pulled off the road and stopped. I got out and walked to the back of the car. Taped on the back window was *February 14,* pictured with a *heart* and a *box of chocolates*; a little creative reminder from my wife. Rushing to the store, I encountered numerous other men pawing through the chocolates. They must have had the same date taped to their back window.

There is a rare breed of men who seem to remember every important date. But they are extremely hard to find. I was fortunate enough to see one on display at our local museum.   He was discovered at a nearby archeological dig. I think he dated back before my time. He was still holding a box of dried chocolates and petrified flowers.   The cause of death was head trauma; a blow to the head from another important date.

This is why I'm thankful my wife keeps track of all this...like **Cow Appreciation Day**. I would forget that day every year if it wasn't for my wife.   Even then, I have trouble sending a cow flowers, considering the run-ins I had with them as a kid.

It's hard enough keeping track of all the important dates, but even more elusive is the perfect gift. It's this elusiveness that causes my anxiety level to reach critical mass. As soon as I enter a store in search of the perfect gift, I'm like a deer in headlights. I don't know which way to go. I give a body fake one way, then the other. Not knowing which way to run, I freeze, and immediately become an ornament on someone's shopping cart. One day I expect to find myself mounted on someone's wall, over their mantle, still peering through the cart.

"That's an unusual rack. Where did you bag him?"

"In the mall; I was hunkered down behind a 'clothes blind.' He walked around the 'blind' and froze. My cart hit him square-on."

For the good part of my life I've been chasing the perfect gift. It's always in the back of my mind. But it's so far back, my memory is either late arriving, or refuses to make the long trek. It could be afraid of the dark.

Shortly after marriage, my wife realized my memory was not in good working order, so she gave me this advice: *"It's the thought that counts."* It was great advice. Thoughts are so inexpensive, and there is no crowding, and pushing and shoving at checkout. So I began sorting through them. I wanted to give my wife the perfect *"thought."*

On the first special occasion, I gave her one of my *thoughts.* She gave me a piece of her mind. Apparently, the thought I gave her didn't count. "No," she said, "When I say "It's the thought that counts," I mean you don't have to look for a big, expensive gift, just something small and inexpensive. Well, not too inexpensive, just something that shows you're thinking about me.

So on **"Get Out of the Doghouse Day,"** I looked for a gift that would fit into the *"thoughts that count"* category. After days of frantically rummaging through purses, fine jewelry, high-fashioned accessories, and some nice *"thoughts"* in several major department stores, I found a refrigerator magnet. I was hoping my *"thought"* would count. It did. It was our first magnet as a married couple. We stood, hand-in-hand, admiring it on the refrigerator.

For her birthday, I got Connie a large bouquet of flowers. "These are beautiful." she said. "Where did you find them?"

"In the neighbor's yard," I answered. "*'Thoughts that count'* require much more creativity."

One Christmas I was sitting in my recliner, staring out the window, shopping for some new thoughts, when my attention was drawn to an article in a popular magazine that said it might not be the *"thought that counts."* I was immediately thrown into a state of confusion, a state where I had once sought residence. Do my thoughts count? Or don't they count. What if I kept my thoughts to myself? Would they count? Who would even know?

To sort out the matter, I decided to read the article. I discovered a person can give the wrong gift. Fruitcakes--a delight of Christmases past--are now on the list of gifts that are unacceptable. So it **ISN'T** the *"thought that counts."* The article stated that a fruitcake is one of the gifts you're mostly likely to get a return on, whether it's returned the day after Christmas or the following Christmas.

After giving it some thought, I returned the Fruitcake I had just received from a friend, informing him that it was no longer in the *"thoughts that count"* category. I hoped it wouldn't mark the beginning of a long, drawn-out Fruitcake War. I didn't want to find any roadside fruitcakes that had to be detonated. Not taking any chances, I bought a fruitcake-sniffing dog.

My friend wrote back, suggesting we call it a rotating *"Trophy Fruitcake."* He would keep it for a year, and then I would keep it for a year. I wrote a reply. "Nice thought," I said, "but I don't think the fruitcake would be up to it. You can keep it." I haven't heard from him in several years. Not taking any chances, I kept the fruitcake-sniffing dog.

Even though my wife insists it's the *"thought that counts,"* I've decided to surprise her for our anniversary this year. Instead of giving her *"thoughts that count"*, I have some *"good intentions."* I hope she likes them. Of course, the biggest problem with *"good intentions"* is that they're hard to wrap. I never have enough wrapping paper.

I had some *"good intentions"* for her birthday, but they got misplaced, and I never did find them. So my body just sat, or reclined; I don't quite remember; whichever was more comfortable.

Fortunately, after a neck adjustment by my wife, an alarm went off, and a message flashed across my brain screen, "**Abandon Recliner, Abandon Recliner!** No, your lifesaver is not under your recliner. It can be found on aisle 12 in the jewelry section at Macy's. You must hurry!"

It's always nice to get some help when you're looking for the perfect gift.

My wife, on the other hand, has no problem with this. Just the other day she announced triumphantly, "I found the perfect gift for you."

"What's the perfect gift?" I asked warily.

"It's an **HPS**," she answered.

"What's an **HPS**?"

"It's a '*Husband Positioning System*.'" It's a terrific little device that can be attached to your belt or suspenders. It gives you the exact location of the clothes hamper, with opening and closing instructions. It also gives directions to the clothes closet, with instructions on how to hang your clothes, how to fold and place your clothes in your drawer. There are directions to other exotic locales as well, such as the garbage, washer and dryer, and the dishwasher, not to mention the vacuum cleaner, duster, and various other handy tools. It will even re-calculate if you miss your turn and walk by garbage that needs to be taken out."

"Wow, you can't beat those features."

"Yes, and it even warns you if there are distractions ahead, such as a ballgame on TV, or a fishing pole calling your name."

Personally, I love a good distraction now and then. Nevertheless, I agreed to try this new gadget. I was surprised by the voice giving instructions. It sounded like the voice of my wife. Wherever I went, the voice would say, "Distraction ahead. Make a U-turn right now. There is a better way." I finally turned off the **HPS** and picked the distraction of my choice.

"How do you like it?" my wife asked the next morning.

"I'm afraid the technology is far beyond most husbands," I answered.

"I guess I'll have to return it and get my money back," said my wife, disappointingly.

"While you're doing that, I'm going to take this old fishing pole out to the lake, and see if it has any fish left in it," I said as I jumped in the car and sped away.

Life was good again. I was enjoying the perfect gift.

Calorie Wars

I've always thought it would be great if weight loss was as simple as letting air out of an over-inflated tire; just a brief hissing sound and presto!...back at your ideal weight! But it was never meant to be simple. It was meant to be warfare.

With the beginning of a New Year, I'm hearing that familiar battle cry..."*This year I'm going to lose weight!*" Prepare for war, because calories will not leave without a fight. Some of you have fought this battle. Even I am a war-tested veteran.

Just the other day, I was out for a walk and became temporarily disoriented. By the time I got my bearings, I found myself standing in an ice cream shop. Without warning, I was attacked by a gang of calories. It may have been two or three gangs. I tried to fend them off, but I was no match for all of them. Before I could break free, I had sampled every flavor. On the way home I watched with a wary eye for another possible ambush.

In my youth, I could burn a truckload of calories daydreaming. They were my friends. I would turn over rocks looking for them. I could always find them at Grams'. It was *Calorie Central*. "Eat, eat, eat," she would repeatedly tell my cousins and me. So we ate, ate, ate...biscuits and gravy, and bacon with an extra side of grease. Lard was a delicacy. The calories complained of overcrowding.

At Grams', overeating was more than a requirement; it was a tradition. Anything less gave the family a bad name. Getting up from the table under your own power meant you hadn't eaten enough. That could mean exile to **Blue Goose Bucksnort**. So I did my part to keep tradition alive.

Years later, I was still trying to keep tradition alive. One day I walked into my favorite lunch stop. Calories saw me coming. They prey on the weak and unsuspecting. I was weak, but I suspected something. 1700 calories were hiding in my double meatball, marinara-slathered sandwich. As soon as I let my guard down, I was assaulted. It was a pathetic sight. The sandwich had to be pulled off me.

Calories, who were once my friends, were suddenly turning on me. They used to burn so easily. Now I couldn't get them lit. I was dealing with an aggressive, new strain that was burn-resistant. I began to collect them. Weight made a house call. I slammed the door. It was the beginning of the *"Calorie Wars."*

I tried to change my ways, but calories would call me in the middle of the night. "We know where you are," they would whisper. "We know how to find you. There you are." I had to wrap the entire refrigerator with duct tape.

If I kept putting on weight, I would have to serve the calories with a restraining order.

Finally, the day of reckoning arrived. (I hate days of reckoning.) I had my picture taken for the local newspaper. The photographer had to take a panoramic shot to get all of me. I would have to start leaving food behind. My wife agreed. "You look much better in x-rays," she said.

"Good," I responded. "Maybe next year we can do a family x-ray that we can send out with the Christmas letter."

Not long after my wide-angle shot, I bumped into my friend, Ralph, at the mall, almost knocking him to the floor.

"You okay?" I asked.

"I'm fine," he answered, "but you should think about getting some exercise."

"I don't mind thinking about it, as long as I don't have to make a commitment."

Ralph loved to jump rope. One day he gave it to me while I was relaxing by his pool. "Here, why don't you try skipping this rope?" he asked.

"I think I **will** skip it."

"No, no, why don't you jump rope?"

"Can't you read my t-shirt? No jumping or skipping allowed. I might be able to step over the rope if it was lying on the ground. But, for safety reasons, my body has banned all jumping and skipping." So I politely declined.

Being a friend, he insisted. "Listen, you just sit by the pool all day. You never go in the water. A little exercise would be good for you."

"Okay, okay," I said. "Give me the rope." I grabbed the rope at both ends, put it behind me, then brought it over my head and jumped. As I was in mid-air, I looked down; there was my stomach. It hadn't left. In the next instant, my body snapped back like a rubber band, colliding with my stomach with such force that it sent me sprawling. "Are you okay?" asked Ralph, running over to help me pick up all my calories that had spilled on the pavement.

"I think I'll be okay if you can just carry me into the house, and let me rest in your recliner. Yeah, that's good. Say, could you turn on the baseball game, and bring me a slice of pizza? I'm feeling much better now."

With the arrival of winter, I thought I had escaped any thoughts of exercise. Then my wife turned on me. You're looking a little pale," she said one day. "I don't think you're getting enough exercise.

"Are you collaborating with Ralph?" I asked.

"No, not at all," she answered. "I just thought you would feel better with a little exercise."

"Well, I'm not jumping rope."

"You don't have to jump rope. Why don't you try cross-country skiing?"

"Okay, okay, maybe. Let me think about it, and I'll let you know in July."

"You know there won't be any snow then."

"I know. I thought that would be the best time."

"I still think you would feel better with some exercise."

I finally decided to try cross-country skiing. Almost immediately, my color returned. My cheeks were rosy, and the rest of my body was black and blue.

One of the first lessons you learn when cross-country skiing is how to stop, probably because that's what you're always trying to do. To stop, you use a method called snowplowing, where you point your toes together, so your skis form the shape of a "V." Although this is intended to slow you down and eventually bring you to a stop, I've used it primarily for clearing obstacles out of my path, such as snow banks, brush, and other skiers. This may be why they want to outfit my skis with cleats.

Next they teach you the art of falling which I picked up quickly, having mastered it years before without skis. Falling is a remarkably simple technique, which is normally done in one motion; in the "blink of an eye." I stand for several seconds before I go into my fall. After completing the fall, I check all my body parts. If everything is still attached, I get up and practice some more, being careful to space my bruises evenly. Although falls can be quite repetitious, it will help you master this art.

During the brief time you're actually standing upright on the skis, you're taught how to move smoothly over the snow, using the "*slide and glide*" method. I found I was much better at the "*split and sit.*"

One note of caution: Never accept any flattery, such as "You're doing very well," while standing in the upright position. This is cause for an immediate "*split and sit.*"

You're also given two poles with your skis. They are perfect for getting started. You stick them into the ground (preferably, one on each side of you), lean forward, give a push, and you're off. You'll be amazed at how a small decline in slope, barely detectable with the naked eye, will make you feel like you're going full speed down the side of a mountain. This is the time to get rid of your poles. In the lessons, they tell you to use your poles to slow down. That's a lie. Drop them. You'll need both hands free for grabbing branches, people, or anything else to help break your speed. See you at the bottom.

During your final lesson, you learn how to get up since, next to stopping, this is what you spend most of your time doing and, next to stopping, it's the most difficult. In fact, the trail is still littered with many of last winter's skiers who were never able to get up.

Cross-country skiing proved to be a terrific weight-loss program. I found I could burn several hundred calories just trying to stand up. Once I got going, the calories were jumping off my body, probably out of fear.

"What am I going to do when I can't cross-country ski?" I wondered. Then I remembered that the **CDC** (*Center for Disease Control*) had just come out with a report saying adults weren't exercising enough. I decided to look at their recommendations. After all, I wanted to be on the cutting block, I mean, cutting edge of something, anything!

The **CDC** study concluded that moderate intensity activities include playing with children; raking the lawn; walking at a brisk pace; playing in a marching band and moderate housework such as scrubbing floors, washing windows, vacuuming; ballroom dancing; and shoveling snow. I must admit, I didn't realize moderate housework would include ballroom dancing, but then again, our home doesn't have a ballroom floor.

For those who are overwhelmed by even moderate exercise, the **CDC** has a list of even less intense activities it says would be at least a step in the right direction, including making photocopies, playing video games, coloring, sitting in a whirlpool bath, floating, and purposeless wandering. They say an hour of this light activity is equal to thirty minutes of moderate activity.

Why stop there? I asked myself. Why not crank it up a couple notches to intense activity? I reasoned; if one hour of light activity equals thirty minutes of moderate activity, two hours of light activity should equal thirty minutes of intense activity. It's been a tremendous success! Now I color for an hour, or until the crayon disappears; then I make photocopies until my two hours are up, stopping occasionally to catch my breath. If I run out of paper, I wander without purpose the remainder of my time. I feel so much better. Although it wasn't included, I think putting one foot forward would also qualify as light activity, and could be included in your exercise regimen.

The **CDC** study failed to mention one activity I'm sure would qualify as an intense activity: listening to a screaming five year old. I didn't realize you could burn up so many calories just listening to someone scream, but it's an excellent weight loss program, in itself. After thirty minutes of screaming, I recommend two days of bed rest. This will give your nerves a chance to heal.

Doing a lot of travel, I've tried to do things on the road to stay in shape. Dodging the traffic works quite well.

I've also tried to take advantage of the exercise rooms in our hotels. Many of these rooms have a full-length wall mirror which makes it appear there is two of everything. One evening I decided I would ride the exercise bike, so I got ready, ran down, and jumped on the one in the mirror. I bruised both knees and several ribs. I thought I was alright, but my body didn't like it. Now, every time I get ready to go exercise, my body fights back, telling me to get a bowl of ice cream and sit down with the remote. I try not to listen.

My good friend, Russell Sprout, told me about a thing called *Visualization*. "You can actually 'visualize' weight loss," he said.

"It's much easier visualizing a buffet," I answered.

Russell went on to explain how weight loss is really in the mind.

"I know it hasn't been down here," I said, pointing to my stomach.

"Just visualize yourself on the treadmill," Russell continued.

So I began visualizing myself on the treadmill. After a short while my heart rate was up and I was starting to pant. Suddenly, I stopped.

"What's the matter?" asked Russell.

"Somebody else wants a turn," I answered.

"Maybe Visualization isn't for you."

"Now I think you're getting the picture."

Everyone is looking for that revolutionary weight loss program. I think I found one that's better than Visualization. I went in to update my driver's license recently. While there, the examiner told me, "I've had people come in here weighing 350 pounds, but their license says 170."

I thought about it for a moment, and then said, "Take twenty off mine, and add a couple inches to my height. I've always wanted to be taller, and I already feel better with the weight off."

ADJUSTING TO CHANGE

As I've already mentioned in a previous chapter, our family once lived in an old 1930's farmhouse. Our children were thankful it was only once. It was a hands-on experience in pioneering. They would have preferred reading about it in a history book.

The farmhouse provided our family with experiences that would last a lifetime, although we usually hoped they wouldn't last through the end of the day. It shaped us into the family we are today...afraid of old farmhouses.

I knew there would be challenges, but rugged individualism would pull us through each challenge. Hopefully, we would find someone with rugged individualism.

During the first winter, we stayed warm by fighting for position around the woodstove. When rugged individualism failed to show, we went in favor of whimpering and whining. We couldn't ignore the frost on the sofa. We were living in an icebox. Still, we were determined to hang on until our story of survival appeared in *Reader's Digest*.

The challenges provided excellent opportunities for building character. It would have been much easier building snowmen.

The farmhouse had few modern features. Actually, I don't think it had that many. We were thankful it had running water.

The kids learned many valuable lessons, which still cause them to suffer from bouts with depression. They learned how to cut and stack a small forest for the woodstove, our only source of heat. They also learned how to identify freezer burn on exposed skin; how to identify the different species of birds in the house; how to scrape enough frost off the sofa, to melt and use for bath water, and how to twirl a plunger like a baton.

Once the kids were grown and out of the house, my wife and I decided it was time to build a new home. With two heat sources gone, we didn't think we could survive another winter.

We knew it would be an adjustment exchanging water views; from the septic tank to cruise ships passing daily on the horizon. Then there would be the spectacular sunsets, and the elk grazing nearby. Like our son said, "It was an adjustment for the Beverly Hillbillies when they moved to Hollywood."

The home was our Christmas present to each other after 20 years of challenging "**Little House on the Prairie**" as the most watched show in town.

I talked about building our new home myself, but my wife said her memories of my remodeling were still fresh in her mind. "I'm still suffering from flashbacks of a toilet spending the summer in the living room," she said. "Oh... and there was that missing molding from Mindy's bedroom that you used as fascia for the roof." She suggested we follow the old Swedish proverb..."If you want something done right, let someone else do it."

So we met with a builder and laid out our plans for a new "*dream*" home. After going over our plans, he gave us the estimated cost of our "*dream*." It was a nightmare. We had visions of grasping at loose bills as they swirled around us.

We decided to trim the "*dream*." After scaling down, we were left with a foundation and a port-a-potty. I asked how much it would be for an extra porta-a-potty. The builder laughed. It was apparent we would have to spend a bit more.

We finally came up with a plan. Then the plan had to be finalized. This is called the Point of No Return. It's where the "real" money is

163

made in building. Any changes made after a prescribed date means you will need to print more money, or live in the walk-in closet, and rent the remainder of your home to someone who can afford to live there.

Within the cost of building, you have allowances for lighting, flooring, cabinets, cement work, appliances, etc. Anything you want is more than the contractor has allowed for. I asked him if there was a living allowance. "No," he answered. "If you want to actually live in the house, you will have to give me more money."

Our lighting allowance was just enough to cover the garage. Any lights in the house were extra. So I started pricing candles. We finally went with the hanging flashlights. My wife doesn't like jumping up to turn off a moving switch, but her timing is improving greatly.

Our new home came complete with climate control. We had climate control in the farmhouse, but it controlled us. In our new home, we controlled the climate. It didn't take us long to adjust to this change.

During the planning, the builder asked, "Would you like a 50, 100, or 150-box garage?"

"We would really like a two-car garage," I answered.

"I've rarely seen a car in a garage; it's usually boxes. The car is always up the street. You take a taxi to the house."

As it turned out, he had keen insight. Once the house was built, we had boxes piled throughout the garage. "Where's the car?" my wife asked one day.

"Up the street," I answered. "I just caught a cab to the house."

"I think it's time we get rid of these boxes. If there *was* a car in here, we would never find it. Anyway, most of these boxes are junk."

"They're another man's treasure," I responded.

"Well, if we're going to get a car in here, you'd better find that man and tell him to come and get his treasure."

When you move into a new home, there is always an adjustment period. It was no different for us. After living in the farmhouse, it took us about three seconds to adjust.

Still, I wanted to make our transition as smooth as possible.

Because we had lived along a busy highway, I knew we would miss the road noise. Fortunately, I was able to get a great recording before we moved. I put it on a CD. When we went to bed, I turned it on. We fell asleep listening to screeching tires, honking horns, some great compression braking, along with an assortment of boom boxes on wheels in surround sound.

We were also serenaded every night by nearby coyotes. But they couldn't compete with the compression braking.

Another farm tradition that I knew we would miss was the annual "*Pipe-burst*", held each winter under our house. It would start with a pipe bursting, and spraying water in the utility. From there, it would spread under the house. What fond memories! We enjoyed so many get-togethers with the local plumber. Connie would always make pipe wrench-shaped cookies for him

"With all the insulation in our new home, I'm afraid we'll miss the *Pipe-burst*," I told my wife.

"Maybe we could take out enough insulation to expose some pipes in time for a cold blast, "she answered. "Otherwise, it could be a very quiet winter."

"Yeah, it would be nice to get together and freeze a few pipes for old time's sake."

In another effort to make our move easier, I petitioned the city to have our septic tank at the farm moved to a sacred spot on our new property. I thought the tank with a golden plunger mounted on top would be a nice memorial. After all, I had invested a good part of my life in the old tank. I had even planned to set aside one day a year, where we would stand by the tank, (holding our breath, of course), in a moment of silence. Sadly, the city denied my petition. Apparently, there was no precedent for a septic tank memorial. I guess you could say the city threw a plunger into my plans.

What we would probably miss the most was "mole town." At the farm, we had cultivated a nice-sized "mole community" in our front yard. We had watched the community grow. We knew many of the moles by name. There was Bob, and Fred, and Digger, to name a few. We were just beginning to attract tourists. I had even printed up brochures, marketing our moles on the same level as the prairie dog towns of South Dakota. If we would have been there one more year, I'm certain we would have made National Geographic. Before we left the farm, I tried to secure a "starter" mole for our new home, but without success. I guess it's just as well. You hate to break up established mole families.

After being in our new home for several months, I was walking through our yard one day and discovered Fred and Digger had returned. I didn't realize moles had a homing instinct. It was good to see them back.

We also had an elk herd that would visit frequently. We liked the elk, but they were hard to mow around.

Even though we were no longer in the farmhouse, we would always carry the millstone, I mean memories, of drapes rustling in a strong wind, power outages, frost on the sofa, a bat hanging in the utility, a bird sanctuary in our daughter's bedroom, and a septic tank backed up to the Canadian border.

Once our home was built, it was time to landscape. If I would have thought about that before we built, I would have stayed in the farmhouse. Everything was on a bank. Most of my time was spent keeping my balance. I could see I was overmatched. So I read an article in a magazine called "Taming the Slope." It would have been easier taming a cornered badger. We finally decided to go with an inexpensive, natural look; something that wasn't pretentious; something that would irritate the neighbors. So we went with the weeds. We liked them. They required little maintenance. We threw in a few dandelions for color. We added a few flowers for the deer, which they enjoyed immensely.

If there are any of you that are interested in building a new home, I would be happy to act as your consultant. I can help you with the necessary adjustments in making your transition a smooth one. I also have some great landscaping ideas.

Listen to Your Body

I'm not certain when the transition took place, but at some point in life I began dressing like an "old man."

I know this to be true because every morning when I get dressed, my wife will ask, "Are you going to wear those clothes?"

"No, I was just putting on a fashion show."

"Well, those are definitely out of fashion. They look like 'old man' clothes."

I have no idea what "old man" clothes look like, but my wife can spot them from a hundred yards in a thick fog.

Having been in the clothes section of Macy's on numerous occasions, I've never seen the section for "old men." So I have no idea how "old man" clothes got into my wardrobe.

I'm just thankful I can still dress myself, although that could change quickly if I don't learn to identify "old man" clothes, and find something else to wear.

All of this has prompted me to work harder at maintaining a youthful appearance. But in my effort to look younger, I've learned it was much easier when I was sixteen; and less costly.

After pricing wrinkle removers, face lifts, hair transplants, tummy tucks, and baggy pants, I now know why people are aging; they can't afford to maintain youth.

Growing up, I never gave much thought to aging. I figured I could do that when I was older and had more time.

Then I got older, and learned that time was short. Desiring to maintain my youth, I decided to join the war on aging. Before I could join, aging declared war on me. It was ruthless. First was the hair. It began disappearing. My comb didn't want to get out of his pocket, feeling as though it was a waste of time trekking through so few hairs each morning. I tried to track down the missing hair.

"Have you seen any hair around the house that matches mine? I asked my wife.

"There was some hair in the car, but I think it belonged to someone else," she answered.

Soon I noticed more hair was missing. I began a frantic search for the hair. I looked in the closet, under the bed, behind the bookcase, on shelves---anywhere you would normally find hair hiding. It was nowhere to be found.

"Maybe it's clinging to life in the shower drain," said Connie.

I put my ear to the drain, trying to hear pleas for help. Not a sound. I tore the drain apart---no hair.

"Maybe it gave up and let go," said my wife.

Not one to give in to hair loss, I checked several combs and an old hairbrush to see if any hair had gotten caught and was struggling to get free. I found plenty of hair in the old hairbrush, but it wasn't mine. It was much older.

I could see the war on aging was going to be a long, drawn-out war. I might have to call in more troops.

After the flight of the hair, came the wrinkles. They totally ignored the "No Trespassing" sign. I tried some wrinkle remover, but they fought it off. I tried scrubbing. They wouldn't budge. I decided against the steam iron.

Without my permission, the wrinkles began inviting their friends. I didn't know if there would be enough room for all of them. They appeared like giant waves rolling in off the ocean. My cheeks began to look like the site of the North Shore Surfing Championship. I could almost feel someone surfing the tube on the side of my face.

"How can I get rid of these wrinkles?" I asked my wife.

"Duct tape," she answered. "Pull your skin back and duct tape it behind your neck. If you wear a turtleneck, no one will notice."

"What a great idea!"

"Just don't yawn," she continued. "You might cause a tsunami. Wrinkles coming back at that speed could break your nose."

To outwit aging, I was going to have to use all the tricks I had up my sleeve. Then I realized I was sleeveless; I would have to take a different approach.

I knew there was a secret to aging gracefully, to looking sixteen when you're actually sixty-seven. I just had to find the secret. If I didn't, aging would stomp all over me. I decided to seek out my chiropractor, Miss Slimmer. I knew she could give me some good advice for maintaining my youth.

Why are you here?" she asked with a cynical laugh. "You never ask me for advice."

I'm trying to find the secret to aging gracefully; to looking sixteen when I'm actually sixty-seven," I said. After giving her time to get up from the floor, where she had crumbled in a heap of laughter, I continued. "Besides, I'm writing this book and..."

"Oh, alright," she said, "I just hope my advice isn't falling on deaf ears."

"Not at all," I answered. "I've just had my hearing tested, and the doctor said its fine. I should be able to hear almost anything, even chiropractors."

"If you really want to age gracefully and maintain your youth, you need to tune in and listen to your body, "said Miss Slimmer.

169

"Come to think of it, I *have* noticed more chatter as I've gotten older," I said. "I often hear whimpering and whining. The other night there were a couple screams, and some loud explosions; probably indigestion. Then there was that fight that woke me up.

"Your body is trying to get your attention," Miss Slimmer went on.

After listening to her advice, I understood why it was crucial to tune in and listen to your body. It's so you can hear age coming. If you're not paying attention, age will sneak up and surprise you.

"Yikes! You scared me. I didn't realize you were already here."

If listening to my body will help me to age gracefully, I'm all for it. "Graceful" brings to mind a picture of a ballet, with a young lady gliding effortlessly and swiftly across the stage on her tip-toes. I like this image far more than shuffling through the house, holding on to furniture. Besides, I can't afford to buy more furniture.

Miss Slimmer continued with her suggestions. "If you want to hear your body say nice things, you need to feed it the right food, like fruits and veggies."

"I don't know what I fed it last night, but my wife said if it keeps talking like that, it can set up camp outdoors, some distance away," I answered.

"That's why it's important to eat the right food, "said Miss Slimmer. "You also need to get plenty of exercise. Your body will thank you for it; maybe even send you a nice card."

I went home determined to follow Miss Slimmer's advice.

That afternoon I decided I would work out on the treadmill, and then enjoy some fresh fruit and veggies. Just when I started to step on the treadmill, my body balked. "Forget the treadmill, "it said. "We can do that later." Let's get a bowl of ice cream and a handful of cookies, and go big game hunting."

I strongly resisted the temptation to shorten my life with ice cream and cookies, but my body used temptation to overcome my resistance. Not wanting to create an ugly scene by fighting back, I wisely filled a large bowl with ice cream, grabbed a package of cookies, and went big game hunting. This meant grabbing my remote and tracking down the top football games on the ESPN highlight reel.

Of course, it's almost impossible to track down any football game unless you're in a recliner with a built-in back massager.

As soon as we had successfully completed our big game hunt, I said, "It's time for us to get on that treadmill." My body didn't hear a word. It was sound asleep. I thanked my body. I was almost asleep, too.

The following morning I was struck with a profound truth, which left a small lump on the side of my head. If I was going to follow Miss Slimmer's advice, I would have to take a tougher stand against the will of my body.

Later that week, I decided to walk a couple of miles around the high school track. My body began protesting immediately. "What are we doing?" it questioned loudly.

"Just walking around the track," I answered. "My chiropractor said you would thank me for it; maybe even give me a nice card."

"Are you joking? I don't give cards, but I may consider legal action if we don't slow down."

"Going too slow is not good; faster is better," I continued.

"Sitting is better," my body went on.

"Don't you want to limber up, keep the blood flowing, live longer?" I asked.

"Live longer? This exercise is killing me! I'll live longer if I lie down. Hey! There's a nice spot on the grass. Let's get over there before some other body takes it." My body ran over and slumped to the ground. "Get up!" I demanded. It didn't move.

Miss Slimmer hadn't told me it would be this hard. I was getting more exercise fighting with my body.

After several rounds, I went to my corner, exhausted.

I talked to several men who had fought the same battle. They gave me some excellent advice. "Pay attention," they said. "You'll see that your body is much more receptive to your wife's voice; even responding to the mere sight of her." Their insight was uncanny.

The next morning my wife came into our bedroom while I was still in bed. "Why aren't you up?" she asked.

"I've been trying to get up for the last thirty minutes, but my body keeps saying, 'I just need another fifteen minutes.' I'm glad you walked in," I continued, as I quickly threw off the covers and jumped out of bed. "Those men were right."

"What men? Right about what?"

"Oh, nothing," I answered.

Since that time, I've noticed a similar pattern. When my wife isn't home, my body seems to have problems with simple things around the house. The other day it refused to pick up my clothes on the floor. It would step over them, but it wouldn't pick them up. It sometimes refuses to do other simple tasks, such as taking out the garbage. I've gotten to the point where I don't even fight it.

"I've seen robots do more work," my wife complained one day, as my body rushed to take out the garbage and pick up my clothes.

"That's because their bodies don't talk back," I answered.

Last Saturday, I was relaxing in my recliner, limbering up my thumb for a little channel surfing when my wife walked in. "I thought you were going to clean the garage today," she said expectantly.

"I was just going out the door when my chiropractor told me to go relax in the recliner. Then she had me do some reaching exercises. That's how the channel changer got in my hands. She said if I keep my thumb moving, I won't get that dreaded 'frozen thumb' syndrome."

"She called?" my wife asked with a puzzled look. "And told you all that?"

"No," I said. "She told me to listen to my body, and that's what my body was telling me to do."

Connie came over and put her ear to my stomach.

"What are you doing?" I asked.

"Listening," she answered. "In fact, I think I hear a still, small voice."

"What is it saying?" I asked.

"It's saying, 'You get out of this chair, and go out and clean the garage, or there's no dinner'."

"I'm surprised I didn't hear that," I said as I ran to the garage.

On Monday, Lester stopped for a visit.

"My chiropractor keeps telling me to listen to my body," I told him, "but it rarely agrees with me. It responds much better to my wife."

"Don't be alarmed. That's natural," answered Lester.

"It must be. Yesterday I wanted to go to the coffee shop, but both hands had a death grip on the sofa."

"You'd better release that grip," my wife demanded. "If he doesn't get to the coffee shop, there won't be any peace around here." My hands let go, and off I stumbled for coffee.

I'm glad my wife was home. Otherwise, I would still be clutching the sofa.

"Maintaining youth is much easier when you're sixteen," said Lester.

Meeting the Widow Maker

In October, my wife and I flew back east to visit our son and his family. During our stay, we journeyed into the Adirondacks for a 17 mile whitewater rafting trip down the Indian and Hudson rivers, an idea that took root in Justin.

When he shared his idea with me, I should have listened to that still, small voice that said, "What? Are you out of your mind? Do not try this! You are a disoriented, frail, old man!"

"No, Connie," I answered. "I've got to try this!"

Wanting to know what I was getting into, I went to the outfitter's website to check it out. I saw pictures of rafts gently drifting down the glistening waters of the Hudson River. I could handle that. Then I looked at the cost. That was harder to handle. I asked how much it would be to float downstream on our backs. They laughed.

I checked for age limits. It was nearing the end of the season, so they allowed eight year olds on the river. I figured if an eight year old could do it, an old man could do it. Then again, it might not work that way. I checked to see if they allowed disoriented old men. They laughed. No problem.

When you arrive at the outfitters, you immediately sign a binding legal document which releases the outfitter from responsibility for your death in the *"Widow Maker"* rapids.

Then they hand you a wet suit, life jacket, and helmet. Next, they go over pre-trip safety instructions. After the instructions, you turn in your wet suit, life jacket, and helmet. As you are fleeing to your car, you remember that you have an eight year old with you. You **CAN'T** let him down. More importantly, you have to save face. You have to ride this baby out. After all, rafting is about respect, not survival. You can always throw respect and saving face out the window when you board the raft. Since there is no window, I would just throw them over the edge of the raft. Once you look downstream, you can start thinking about survival.

In the meantime, I have to prove my manhood, even though the chicken in me is squawking fiercely against it. As Tim Allen would say, "This is a man thing." So I rounded up all my nerves and put on a mask of sheer calm. I could take off the mask when I got to the river.

We all watched as several rafts were loaded onto the top of an old, rickety school bus. (Rickety is a requirement for rafting trips.) Once loaded, everyone piled into the bus, laughing and making merry, like everything would be alright.

We were then driven 15 miles into the wilderness. The driver stopped near a wild and raging river. Is that our river!? After my fingers were pried off my seat, I was pulled from the bus. While I was being pulled from the bus, all the guides were removing their rafts. I was hoping we would get a raft that didn't leak. I listened for hissing sounds.

Once you have your raft, your guide gives you more safety instructions, along with various commands he will be sharing with you on your trip down Death River, I mean downstream.

First, he explains the safety line that runs along the outside of the raft. The safety line is also called the *"chicken line."* You grab it in case of emergencies. I consider whitewater rafting an emergency, so I grab the line. I'm not letting go!!

The guide then explains the art of "Anchoring in." He shows you how to anchor your feet while sitting on the edge of the raft. He demonstrates by anchoring his feet and leaning back over the edge of the raft. This will prevent you from being thrown into the "widow maker" rapids. I'm all for anchoring in, but I don't lean that far back in bed. So I practice anchoring in. I get my feet anchored, but I don't lean back. If I do, I will fall overboard, with my feet still in the raft. I need them for walking, so I sit straight up…great posture, but low survival rate.

Note: If your feet are anchored properly, you can fall out of the raft, but your feet will remain anchored. So if you're out swimming around, looking for your feet, they are still in the raft, anchored in.

Before anyone gets into the raft, the guide tells us to pick our position. I ask for the third seat behind the bus driver. But the driver has already left with the bus. Shoot! So I wait for everyone else to pick their position. After the others have staked their claim to a spot on the raft, I take my position…hunkered down on the floor of the raft, covering my head, and praying without ceasing.

Next we're told how to use our oars. Be sure to keep one hand on the end of the oar…not the end that's in the water. You don't want to be swinging the oar and end up breaking the jaw of a raft mate.

Then our guide tells us about the different commands we need to follow; hard right, left back, easy forward, row hard, row hard, lean right, lean left, hunker down, grab the chicken line, swim… Let me ask you this…how does a 67 year old remember all those commands? The only commands I could remember were *"Hunker Down"* and *"Grab the Chicken Line."* And I was doing that before we set the raft in the water.

After a few more words regarding safety, the guide tells me I will need to loosen my fingers from the chicken line, so I can use that hand on the oar. We finally "put in." Then I discover we're in the wrong river. I thought we were rafting the Hudson. I'm told the Indian River will flow into the Hudson in three miles. I hope I live to make the Hudson. Then I discover that we "put in" just below a dam. They do this on purpose; so they can release water from the dam and turn your 2-3 class rapids into a class 5 white knuckle trip, with lots of screaming, ricocheting off rock walls, grabbing for chicken line, and general mayhem. I see this is going to be fun!

Shortly after pushing off, rapids appeared. My eyes widened. "Did the dam break!?" I yelled! "Those rapids have to be a 12." I prayed for the Second Coming before we hit them full force.

"The rapids on the left are called the 'Widow Maker' rapids," our guide yelled. "We want to avoid them." All the rapids looked like "Widow Makers." So I'm rowing hard for land. We can carry the raft to the highway and flag down an old, rickety school bus. But it's too late.

As soon as we hit the rapids, I saw Connie flying home alone. One of the grandkids flashed before my eyes. Spitting out water and opening my eyes, I suddenly realized that one of the grandkids **HAD** flashed before my eyes! Carter had bounced out of the raft. Justin pulled him back in.

While Connie was drinking her hot chocolate at McDonald's, I was drinking from the Indian River, and trying to re-fit my eyeballs into their sockets. I didn't realize fearing for my life could be so much fun!

We had just survived the Widow Maker, but we still had to face *Big Nasty, Satan's Cesspool, Meat Grinder, Old Man Overboard*, and *Killer*—this one is bad. This rapid is so scary, that it's too scary to look at. So you run it backwards. Once you've gotten through these rapids, there are more waiting for you...hunker down and grab the chicken line!

We finally arrived at our destination. The last mile we drifted, which was a good thing. Our wrists were so sore from paddling that they didn't want to take another stroke. Jaxon fell asleep as we drifted.

It was time for reflection. I had resisted that still, small voice, and survived *Big Nasty, Killer*, and the *Widow Maker*. I was glad I had done the rapids. Had I not survived, it would have been a different story. I told Connie I wouldn't trade the experience for anything. "That's because no one would trade with you," she answered.

After the outfitter's served us dinner, we ambled toward the car. As we drove off, I found my arms wanting to row the steering wheel. I started yelling commands like left front, right back. Then I told everyone to grab the chicken line and hang on. Potholes ahead!